instant **expert** • instant **expert** • instant **expert** • instant **expert** •

KNITTING

Thunder Bay Press
An imprint of the Advantage Publishers Group
5880 Oberlin Drive, San Diego, CA 92121-4794
www.thunderbaybooks.com

Series editor: Katy Bevan, MQ Publications
Editorial director: Ljiljana Baird, MQ Publications
Photography: Lizzie Orme
Styling: Catherine Huckerby
Design concept: Balley Design Associates

ISBN 1-59223-345-7
Library of Congress Cataloging-in-Publication Data
available upon request.

Printed in China
1 2 3 4 5 09 08 07 06 05

KNITTING

THUNDER BAY
P·R·E·S·S

San Diego, California

Contents

INTRODUCTION

The aim of this book is to inspire people to take up the fantastic hobby of knitting. This is a craft that began simply as a way of creating clothes for warmth and has become a popular way of making fashionable garments.

In this book, I hope to teach you all the basic skills needed to begin knitting and to inspire and encourage you to continue long after you have completed the projects in this book. Although I have suggested yarns for each pattern, you can replace these with other yarns that appeal to your own style. As long as the new yarns match my suggestions in ply (thickness), the projects will work just as well. This freedom enables you to translate the styles in this book into unique pieces of your own. Once you have gained confidence, you can then go on to develop and explore your own design skills, using the tips and hints given at the end of many of the projects.

As a collector of knitwear—whether in the form of old patterns or classic vintage pieces—I am continually inspired to design new styles of my own. I love the texture of knitwear and its flexibility, and I am always amazed at the incredible skill and creativity that nonprofessional knitters show. I hope that by reading this book, you will learn to share my passion for this beautiful and fulfilling craft.

I have given a brief history of knitting as an introduction. I would, however, like to point out that in my research I came across much contradictory information and the following is my own interpretation based on the information I found. However, as archaeologists continue unearthing our history and as technology advances, new information about the development of knitting may be discovered.

B.BAUCOUR

Publications
François Tedesco,
Paris.

part

1

KNITTING THEN AND NOW

A HISTORY OF KNITTING

It is hard to say when knitting was first discovered and by whom because dating its origin is complicated by the fragile and perishable nature of natural fibers. Knitting in some form has, however, been around since Roman times, and new discoveries of ancient knitted fabrics are being made that add depth to our knowledge of this craft.

Knitting then

Fragments excavated by archaeologists from a Roman-era site dating to 256 at Dura Europas, Syria, were originally considered to be the earliest example of knitwear. They have, however, now been identified as having been created not by knitting but by another technique known as "nalbinding" (also spelled "nålbinding," "naalbinding," and "nalebinding"). This is a method of creating a stretchy fabric with short lengths of yarn and a single-eyed needle. The material is formed by looping the yarn through at least two previously created loops, gradually building up row upon row of loops. As with knitting, the thickness of the fabric depends on the type of yarn being used and the looseness/tightness of the individual nalbinder.

Nalbinding predates both knitting and crochet by at least 2,000 years. Other archaeological finds of toed ankle socks from fifth- and sixth-century Egypt are also examples of nalbinding that were previously wrongly identified as knitting. Nalbinding as a practical needlecraft survived for many years in Scandinavia before being replaced by knitting.

Other scraps of knitted fabric that have been found in Egypt date back to between the seventh and ninth centuries, and it is clear that by then, the Egyptians had attained a high understanding of the craft and were producing elaborate and complex works. One of the earliest fragments of fabric knitted with needles was discovered in Fostat, an ancient Egyptian city. This incredibly intricate piece is said to have around forty-five stitches per inch, and it would have required a high level of skill to produce such a fine and delicate sample of work.

It is thought that the oldest pieces of knitting are some two-color socks made from cotton, dating from thirteenth- to fifteenth-century Islamic Egypt. These fragments show complex two-color patterning in combination with simple stripes and some Arabic script.

The birth of stockinette

Among the eighth- to tenth-century Viking tombs of Norway and northern Scandinavia, fragments of fabrics have been found that show a fusion of weaving and knitting known as "sprang." This method was produced from a series of vertical threads, similar to the warp in weaving, which were set up on a frame. A chain stitch was worked vertically up the first thread, using a simple sewing needle, and a second row was then interlaced with the sides of the first row of chains. When the whole frame was covered, the vertical threads were removed, leaving a fabric very similar to stockinette stitch, although the interlock between the stitches was sideways instead of through the top of the loops, as in knitting.

Below Eighty-year-old Johnny Bear has knitted Cowichan sweaters for half a century. (British Columbia, Canada.)

Above Knitted Fair Isle cap and gloves from the 1940s.

It is not known where sprang originated. Evidence of an early version of sprang was located in excavations of an ancient village in Peru from around 500 BC. Textile fragments have been excavated from Norwegian and Danish peat bogs dating from as early as 1500–1100 BC, which have been identified as caps and stockings. Evidence has also been found of pieces made in Norway, Denmark, and Sweden from the Viking period onward.

Paintings on early Greek vases appear to depict women making a fabric very similar in appearance to sprang. More recently, the method has been used in Mexico, where it is used for shopping bags and hammocks, and in Winnebago, Wisconsin, where the Indians use it to make scarves.

A similar form of knitting to sprang, which dates to the first century, has also been found in Peru. Although it was not worked with two needles, it resembles stockinette stitch even more closely than sprang. It was worked with a basic sewing needle and thread, using a horizontal line of thread as the base. A series of loops was built up along the base row, and a second row of loops was then interlinked with the bases of the first loops; the rows were then continued until the fabric was completed. The finished fabric is known as "Peruvian needle knitting."

The spread of knitting

The oldest samples of knitting from medieval Europe have been identified as two finely knit cushions found in the thirteenth-century tombs of a Castilian prince and princess. (A former kingdom of Spain, Castile comprises the two regions of Old Castile in northwestern Spain and New Castile in the center of the country.)

The beautiful cushions were finely knitted using a complicated two-color pattern that covered the whole area. One also had an Arabic inscription on it. This suggests that knitting may have been transported by the Moors from the Middle East to Europe via Spain. Although this theory is not conclusive, at present it seems the most likely for the dissemination of knitting from the Middle East to Europe.

The elaborate, Arabic-influenced knitting styles the Moors brought were an inspiration for the Spanish and Italian knitting industry, which reached its peak over a thousand years later. Meanwhile, in Austria and Germany, heavily cabled fabrics with embroidery were influenced by Florentine knitwear. In Florence itself, coats were finely worked using silver and gold threads to produce richly brocaded knitted fabrics. Each of these countries would add its own layer of identity to a craft whose history, in the form of looped thread fabrics, can be traced back almost two millennia.

Knitters' guilds

In the Middle Ages, knitted fabrics and clothes were produced by knitters' guilds, which operated across Europe. These guilds were composed of men who had refined this ancient craft and were producing exquisite fabrics for the nobility of the day. Each member of high society would own some precious knitted garments, and they would even have their own personal knitting master to create these unique items of clothing.

To become a member of this elite group of knitting masters, a young man would have to serve a three-year apprenticeship with a master, then spend the same amount of time traveling, where he could learn skills from masters in other countries. He would then return to take an exam, during which he had to produce an original piece of work involving intricate designs and using many colors. After this he could be called a master himself. In turn, he would take on his own apprentices and start the process again, continuing the perfection of the craft.

The guilds were run along very strict guidelines, with stringent regulations to keep the standards high and to prevent poor-quality goods from being produced. If these regulations were violated, the member could lose his job and his livelihood since all sales were also controlled by the guild. In this way, knitters' guilds were self-regulating and that is why the standards were so high wherever these guilds existed.

Sixteenth-century developments

During the reign of Queen Elizabeth I of England (1558–1603), the frame knitting machine was invented. This simple device marked the beginning of the stocking industry in England, which then spread around the world, with England exporting large quantities of stockings.

In fact, it was via a gift of a fine pair of stockings to the king that knitting reached Denmark. The king was so impressed that he invited knitters from Holland to teach Danish women how to knit. However, only the members of his court were allowed to wear the silk stockings that were knitted. Other Danes protested, and it was agreed that other classes could wear stockings too—although the middle classes were permitted only the more humble cotton version, and the peasants were allowed to wear only poor-quality stockings made of rough yarn.

Also during this time, felted knitting was introduced in England. This process of soaking and pummeling knitted woolen fabric, which was thought to have originated in the Basque region of France, was used to produce the French beret. Across the Channel in England, the knitters' apprentices would wear elaborate hats produced from felted knitted fabrics.

An example of sixteenth-century knitting can be found in the New York Metropolitan Museum of Art, where there is a knitted jacket with knit-and-purl patterning, as well as color patterning. The pieces were knitted flat, then sewn together afterward. The difference in the patterns on the front and back may indicate that they were knitted in the same workshop but by different people.

Another example of a flat-knitted garment with knit-and-purl patterning is the blue silk tunic worn by King Charles II to his execution in 1685.

Knitting goes west

With the colonization of the Americas in the early seventeenth century, European knitting traditions spread via missionaries, sailors, and other new arrivals. Depending on the nationality of the immigrants, different knitting traditions were passed on to the Americans, who then developed their own skills. To complete the circle, traditions developed in America eventually crossed the Atlantic with Irish émigrés returning home from America and found their way into the famously intricate sweaters from the Aran Islands.

Women start to knit

The start of the industrial revolution in the late eighteenth century and the introduction of knitting machinery eventually moved the craft away from men and into the home, where it became a productive home-based skill pursued by women. Until that point, women had been allowed only to spin the yarn for the men to knit.

The popularity of knitting as a woman's pastime spread, and by Victorian times it ranked among the skills of the upper classes, alongside playing the piano, painting watercolors, and doing embroidery. Knitting patterns started appearing in the magazines of the day, and these were soon followed by specialty magazines, which proved extremely popular and helped knitting to become a widespread hobby.

Ganseys

During the nineteenth and early twentieth centuries, strong traditional knitting styles developed throughout Europe. One of these traditions was the gansey, which was produced along the British coast, particularly around Cornwall, Guernsey (from where they got their name), Ireland, and the islands of Scotland. Each port produced these heavy, woolen, seamless sweaters, which were knitted in stockinette stitch or made with simple patterns using purl stitch on a stockinette stitch background. Fishermen would wear their ganseys to work in or while fishing, and the individual patterns on the sweaters meant that each fisherman's home port could be identified from his gansey. They would have more complicated patterns for special occasions, using heavy cables, embossed stitches, and bobbles.

It was also a tradition for the women to knit these individual sweaters before marriage and present them to their husbands on their wedding day. (For this reason, these sweaters were sometimes known as "bridal shirts.") The complex nature and individuality of the design showed each woman's love and, of course, her skill with her knitting needles. Some knitters even worked their initials or full name—or even the name of their husband's boat—into the garment above the hem. This personalization was a form of identification that would prove useful in the event of the wearer being found drowned.

The basic gansey is similar throughout Great Britain. Traditionally, the patterns were never written down but were passed from mother to daughter or friend to friend and were constantly being added to. As the fishermen traveled around the country working in different areas doing seasonal work, so the different patterns spread throughout the country.

These gansey sweaters were also knitted commercially, and production reached its peak in the middle of the nineteenth century. A number of similarities may be noted between the gansey and early Italian knitwear from the seventeenth century, and this may be due to the enormous amount of knitwear that was exported from the Channel Islands to Europe in Elizabethan times. The shape is very similar to seventeenth-century Italian silk shirts, although it had been modified to suit the harsher elements of yarn and the need for a man's garment that would stand the rigors of a tough working life.

Fair Isle sweaters

Another tradition was also developing in the remote Shetland Islands, which are a group of over a hundred islands situated between northeast Scotland and Norway, only fourteen of which are inhabited. Legend has it that in 1588 a ship from the Spanish Armada was wrecked off Sheep Rock in the Shetlands. Survivors from the wreck taught the island women the art of colored knitting in return for their keep, copying patterns from the knitwear they were wearing and from the corpses that had washed ashore.

Below Women from the Shetland Islands carding and spinning wool before it is knitted.

red also appear around the 1840s, when they were first imported. After 1920, however, mill-dyed yarns were imported, giving the knitters a wide range of colors to knit with and encouraging knitting as an export.

The original use of these sweaters, as with the ganseys, was as work wear, but in 1921, the then Prince of Wales was seen wearing a Fair Isle sweater while playing golf in Scotland. He then also wore it in a portrait painted by Sir Henry Lander. This inevitably made this style of knitwear very fashionable, and its popularity continued until the 1950s. After that time, the Norwegian patterned sweaters, which used trees, snowflakes, and star images, became more popular. In recent years, however, there has been a revival in knitting in the Fair Isles—fueled by the tourist industry—which it is hoped will continue for many years.

Other styles

Other traditional styles developed around this time were heavily decorated worsted-weight sweaters from the Aran Islands, with their complex use of cables and twisted patterns. In Scandinavia, single- and two-color stranded knitting was developing, while in eastern Europe, the stranded knitting was produced in many colors

Knitting in wartime

During World War I, the need for practical knitwear for the soldiers from both sides of the Atlantic was instrumental in encouraging knitting in the home, as balaclavas, socks, and gloves were essential for the troops. This also happened in World War II, when many knitting pattern books had practical patterns for scarves and other necessities.

Soldiers and sailors had also long been taught and encouraged to knit their own socks and gloves as ways of keeping warm. In World War II, British soldiers imprisoned in Austria knitted socks, caps, and other items of clothing, using yarn supplied by the Red Cross, to keep themselves from freezing to death.

Knitting goes couture

From 1920, the fashion houses of Paris began designing increasing amounts of knitwear to include in their couture collections. The 1920s were definitely a sweater age, and this is the decade that first introduced the "Sloppy Joe"

Above Portrait of HRH Prince Edward, the Prince of Wales, by John St. Helier Lander, 1925.

The earliest example of patterned knitting found on the islands dates to 1680–1690. It was found on the body of a man who had been preserved in a peat bog. He was wearing patterned stockings, a hat, and gloves. It is unknown whether he was an islander or a trader from another country.

A cap and purse knitted in silk, which may have been made for Victorian tourists, are the only other items of Fair Isle patterned knitwear to be found that date before about 1850. It is more likely that the Fair Isle patterns are related to the knitting of Estonia and Russia, and were brought across the North Sea by traders.

The colors used in these patterns of crosses, hexagons, and triangles were mostly natural shades of browns, grays, and creams, which came from the native sheep of the islands. Yellow yarn was also used (it was created by dyeing the yarn using onion skins), and indigo blue and madder (a loose-fitting sweater usually worn by girls), a look that has been revived a few times since then.

Anny Blatt was a leading designer of knitwear at this time, and in the 1930s, her knitting leaflets were published so that home knitters could reproduce the Paris fashions. This revolutionized the knitting styles available to the general public.

Another publication that became popular was *Stitchcraft*. This finally brought fashion and knitwear together for the masses and was available on every newsstand. Many more knitting books began appearing, and although their popularity has waxed and waned over the past fifty years, these influential publications have continued to appear. In fact, more books and knitting magazines have been published in the twenty-first century than ever before, thanks to the number of younger people who have rediscovered the joys of this ancient craft.

Below During World War I, girls on all sides were encouraged to knit at school, making warm socks and other woolen clothing for the troops on the front lines. This knitting class was photographed in Germany in 1915.

KNITTING NOW

As far as the catwalk is concerned, knitting is back in fashion. Over the past few decades, knitting changed from being utilitarian to fashionable, before losing popularity at the end of the last century. Now, however, there is a newfound interest in this versatile craft, and knitwear is again a favorite of clothing designers.

The 1950s

Until the late 1950s, most everyday clothing items could—and would have—been knitted, from socks and underwear to hats and swimsuits and every other item of clothing in between. There was a pattern available for just about everything, and most households counted at least one knitter among its inhabitants. The fact that not many tools were required and that it was easy to knit while chatting made it a very appealing and practical pastime.

In addition, many household essentials had to be knitted since, postwar, there was very little choice in the stores. Blankets and cushions, kitchen necessities such as potholders, washing and floor cloths, and many other items essential to the home at that time could be hand-knitted at home.

For this reason, children in the 1950s were taught to knit at school. All children would be capable of doing a garter stitch from a very young age, and it was not uncommon for children under the age of eleven to be able to knit complex Fair Isle patterns.

The 1960s

During the 1960s, knitting was very fashionable and was an essential skill for young women—and some men—if they wanted to keep up with the fashion trends. Hand-knitted tank tops, leg warmers, socks with separate toes, and mufflers with matching gloves were highly fashionable, and being able to make these things oneself gave great kudos to the wearer.

The 1970s

Crafts such as sewing, embroidery, knitting, and cooking were still taught in schools until the late 1970s, as well as being passed down from generation to generation, mostly from mother to daughter. The decision to drop such practical subjects from the school curriculum resulted in a decline of these skills in the ensuing generations.

In the fashion world of the late 1970s, followers of the new styles were wearing mohair sweaters knitted loosely in bright colors, as seen in early Vivienne Westwood collections.

The 1980s

At the beginning of this decade, knitting was still popular, and using shapes that were strongly influenced by 1940s fitted garments, even shoulder pads in knitwear, was the fashion of the day. In addition, the trademark emphasis of designers such as Edina Ronay was on the use of finer yarns and texture.

Later in the decade, knit styles changed direction again, and the trend was for large picture sweaters. Knitwear designers such as Artwork, Patricia Roberts, and Kaffe Fassett were producing designs using large areas of complicated pattern and color, with the accent being on the pattern. The garment shapes tended to be quite simple, allowing the motifs to be the focus. Also fashionable were 1950s-style zip-up cardigans based on the old Mary Maxim patterns.

There was also a more radical look from the new young designers of the day, such as Body Map, who explored shapes in a way that had not been seen before in knitwear: extending sleeves and playing around with the scale of clothes, distorting them and creating fantastic shapes.

The 1990s

Although knitwear was still much in evidence in the 1990s on the catwalk and in stores, it suffered a huge decline as a hobby. This was the beginning of cheap, mass-produced clothes, when chain stores were closing the gap on designers and starting to reproduce the catwalk styles within months instead of a year.

Throughout this decade, the decline in interest in knitting meant that increasing numbers of yarn stores, craft stores, and notions departments either closed down or were greatly reduced in size.

The value of learning to knit

Being able to knit is a valuable skill in its own right, but the process of learning how to knit has other advantages. It helps young people integrate right- and left-brain learning, improves concentration, and aids dexterity. It has been continually taught in the Rudolph Steiner schools because of these benefits. It is seen as a fun way of aiding mathematical skills, since being able to add, divide, and multiply are fundamental requirements for knitting. Steiner schools even encourage students to make their own needles from waxed wooden dowels. In this way, they are encouraged to take pride in their work from beginning to end, and producing something practical and attractive from scratch gives an overall sense of achievement.

Traditional versus new fabrics

Over the last twenty years, knitwear had been relegated down the ranks of the fashion chain by the development of sports and performance fabrics, which have had a huge influence on fashion trends. People are now realizing, however, that performance fabrics such as fleece do not have the same appeal or shelf life as knitted fabrics made from natural fibers. Materials such as wool or cotton will last much longer and remain in good condition for years if they are looked after. Proof of this longevity may be seen in the vintage clothing now being worn by fashionistas.

Cashmere

The popularity of cashmere over the past few years is also part of the revival in interest in natural fibers. For years the fashionable people who could afford to buy their clothes from couture houses have been hailing the virtues of this wonderful yarn, and now it is more accessible than ever before. Most leading designers will have cashmere somewhere in every collection. Even chain stores now have their own cashmere styles each season.

Traditional Scottish mills and makers of fine, exclusive knitwear, such as Pringle and Lyle & Scott, who have been in business for decades, have seen a boom in their sales due to this newfound interest in luxury yarns. Cashmere is lighter and softer than almost any man-made yarn and warmer than any comparable material.

Designers such as Fake London have also been part of an eco-friendly trend that recycles cashmere and hand-knitted Aran sweaters, restructuring them so that we can appreciate their intrinsic value once more. These updated styles are then shown alongside traditionally made cashmere knitwear in the same fashion collections.

Designers that produce these fabulous garments show that even those of us who cannot afford them can be inspired to achieve the same look ourselves with a bit of effort and a basic knowledge of knitting.

The joy of knitting

There are now books that extol the virtues of simple living, and knitting fits very well into this way of thinking. An organization called the "Slow Movement" encourages crafting as the means of gaining inner fulfillment. In an age when people spend hours in front of computer screens at home or work and travel on busy trains and buses, the slow, monotonous process of knitting can be both meditative and relaxing. Simply working on something for the pleasure of it—having a creative outlet—is extremely important in a fast-moving world.

The repetitive process of knitting can also provide stress relief, and some knitters believe that their state of mind is apparent in their work. When they are relaxed, their knitting appears smooth and effortless, but if they are tense, their work shows an uneven quality. The rewarding feeling of creating something for oneself or as a gift is also hugely satisfying. Handmade items have a rare value in today's society. Their charm is in the imperfections or handmade quality and gives profound pleasure to both maker and receiver.

Being interested in knitting shows an appreciation of handicrafts. It is also a way of stating one's individuality and refusing to be categorized by one's clothes. Through knitting you are creating your own designer heirlooms that will last and last. You will not be disappointed with the huge selection of patterns now available: they are all out there, waiting.

Organized knitting

Knitting groups and clubs are now popping up everywhere, in towns and cities and on university campuses; some schools and youth organizations are even offering classes for children. Over the last few years, it is thought that four million newcomers in the Western world have discovered knitting and taken it up as a new hobby, and young professionals can now be found meeting in cafés and bars to indulge in this ancient pastime.

A spirit of generosity exists in these groups, where people swap patterns, share yarns, and offer each other tips and advice. An extreme example of this was a group that got involved with collecting thirty-two tons of yarn from knitters all around the United States, which they then distributed to women in the former Yugoslavia for creating garments. The women benefited financially from the sale of the sweaters, but there were emotional gains too, as the women talked together while knitting, helping to heal the scars of war.

There are now hundreds of Web sites that offer advice, tips, free patterns, and other information about the craft, many with links to chat rooms aimed at enthusiasts.

Knitting in the twenty-first century

Designer knitwear can be seen on every catwalk this season and is highly influential at the moment. Recent editions of *Vogue* and other magazines show page after page of designer knitwear that encompass all styles and use a wide variety of techniques. There are huge, oversized cardigans from Chloe, fitted fine cashmere knits from Prada, bulky cable knits from John Rocha and Eley Kishimoto, and multicolored striped wraps from Missoni and Junya Watanabe. Half of the new up-and-coming designers are using knitwear as the focus of their collections. The future for knitting looks very bright.

Right Knitted ensemble by Missoni, spring/summer 2004, Milan, October 2003.
Below Fashion models at a knitting party at Knit New York, February 2004.

part

2

BASICS

YARNS

There is a huge selection of knitting yarns available, and as long as your gauge matches the one on your pattern, you could use any one of them. When choosing a yarn for a particular garment, however, it is important to look not just at the color but also at the different qualities of the various yarns. Remember that the thickness of yarn in differing brands may vary, and this is why knitting a gauge swatch is so important (see page 29).

You should have no difficulty finding a yarn that you like. Numerous companies make knitting yarn, although department stores tend to stock their own brands and a small selection of the most popular makes. Try to find a local supplier, which will carry a much larger selection and will have expert salespeople to give you advice.

Alternatively, you can buy your yarns online. The Internet is an amazing resource for a huge selection of unusual, quality yarns, from silk and angora to mohair, rayon, and, of course, wool and cotton. Through the Internet you can gain access to individual dyers and spinners, who will generally be able to ship to anywhere in the world. This is certainly a great way of ensuring an individual garment by finding an unusual yarn in both texture and color.

Hard-wearing yarns are good for outdoor clothes or some children's wear. Cotton is hard-wearing, and, being smooth, it is good for children who often do not like the scratchy feel of some wools. A downside to cotton yarns, however, is that they can stretch. For very young children and babies, soft and fine yarns would be good for clothes or shawls, and are also good for scarves using lace stitches.

Whatever type you choose, it is best to work with good-quality yarns. After all, the time that you spend on your work deserves the best materials, and it would be very disappointing if after one wash your garment looked old and tired.

Experimenting and getting used to the appearance of different yarns adds an exciting dimension to your work. To make up a pattern in a completely different yarn from the one suggested will greatly change the appearance of the garment to create something unique, and this is an inspiring aspect of any creative work. For example, a fingering weight mercerized cotton garment will have a very different look than a fingering weight mohair one, even though the gauge may be the same.

Types of yarn

There are numerous mixes of yarn fibers available in addition to wool and cotton. Mixes of wool and silk, cotton and linen, and synthetic fibers with both cotton and wool are just a small selection of what is available. As with all creative work, researching and trying things out is the way to find the yarns you like to work with.

Different yarns also give hugely differing results: smooth or rough, silky or hairy, short filaments or long. Certain yarns are also more elastic than others. Wool generally tends to have more flexibility than cotton, and a linen yarn will be very durable (although, unless mixed with cotton, it can be rough). However, all yarns have a purpose, and the strength of a linen thread makes it perfect for a bag that will have lots of strain put on it.

Rayon yarns and ribbon-type yarns can have a sheen that really cannot be found in other yarns, and these glittering qualities can be very effective in a finished garment. However, a beginner may find it difficult to work with such a slippery yarn.

Some of the yarns available today are wool, cotton, silk (matte or shiny), linen, ribbon, slub, bouclé, and chenille. All can be bought in stores or by mail order, and once you have become confident in your knitting, it is worth experimenting with and learning about the various qualities of the many different fibers. Yarn usually comes in 2-oz. balls, although 4-oz. balls are also available in many

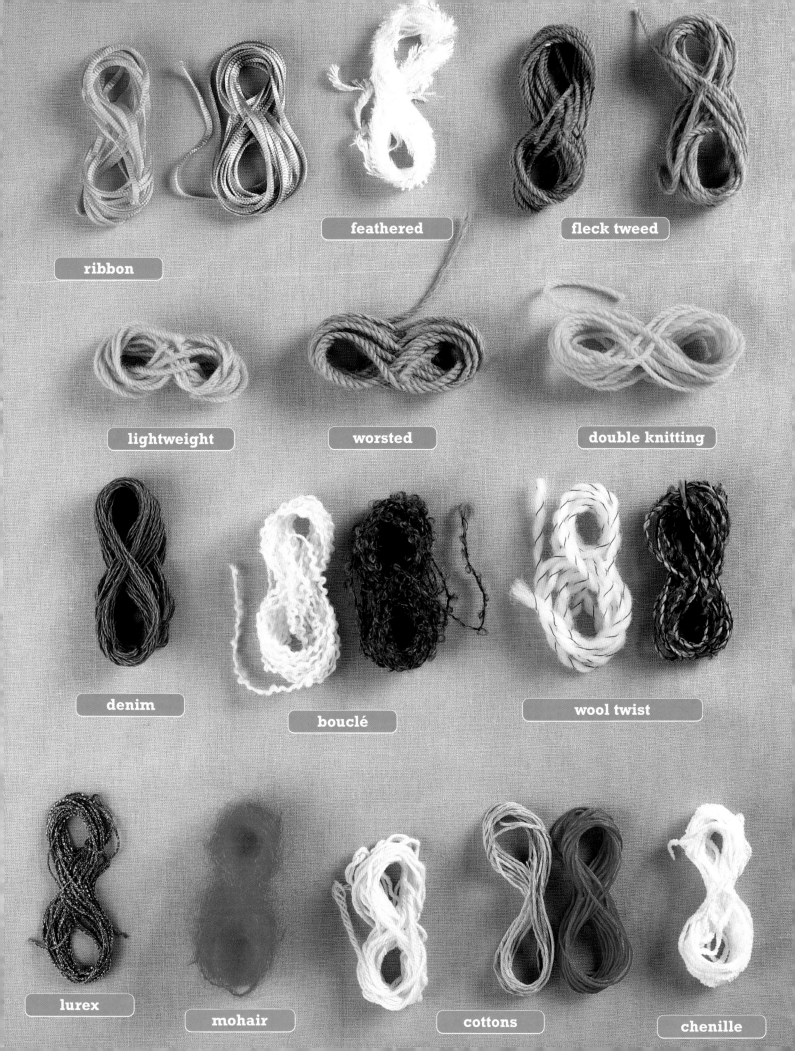

ribbon

feathered

fleck tweed

lightweight

worsted

double knitting

denim

bouclé

wool twist

lurex

mohair

cottons

chenille

brands. It is unusual to find 1-oz. balls these days, except from some specialty producers of cashmere and angora.

Skeins of yarn are still produced by small dye companies, but buying these will necessitate winding the skein into balls. You can buy equipment for doing this, but unless you are planning a lot of knitting, the old-fashioned method of two hands and a chair back is still the best (see below for instructions).

Dye lot

All knitting yarns will have a number on the ball band or inside the cone; this relates to the batch in which it was dyed. It is essential to check this number when purchasing yarn, making sure that all your balls are from the same batch. Although it may not be obvious at this stage, any yarn from a different dye vat will definitely show when the garment is finished.

Winding on a bobbin

When working in intarsia or Fair Isle, you will need small amounts of the contrast colors. To keep the yarn from tangling, make small wrappings of yarn: Using the thumb and little finger, wrap the yarn in a figure eight to the desired amount. Break off from the main ball and then secure the end around the center of the bundle. This method should keep the wrap in shape and prevent

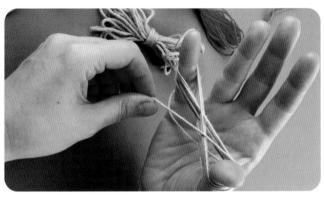

tangling. Use the yarn from the center of the bobbin first. If using lots of colors in a row, it can be useful to have each separate color in its own small bag or even a jar; this will enable you to control the yarn. Plastic bobbins are also available or you can make your own from cardboard—these are good for use with very fine fibers.

Skeins

Occasionally, yarn still comes on skeins, especially from small specialty dyers. There is a tool available, called a "knitter's umbrella," that unfolds, allowing you to place the skein onto it. This will then turn as you wind off your yarn into a ball. However, they seem to be harder to come by these days so you may have to resort to the age-old method of using another pair of hands or a chair back to hold the skein while you wind a ball.

A ball winder is also available in some specialty stores; it enables you to wind a ball in the shape of a squat cylinder. When removed from the winder, you can take the yarn from the center to prevent tangles.

TOOLS

Let's begin with the tools of the trade—yarn, needles, and other essentials. Once you have gathered some of these materials, you will need a knitting bag to keep them all together, as they will soon accumulate. You may also want a small bag with a zipper, for the small tools.

Needles

Knitting needles come in different sizes and are usually straight and made from steel, plastic, or wood. Bamboo needles are also generally available. Although wooden needles are probably the most attractive, they are not as strong as either steel or plastic. If buying them, choose a good-quality brand to avoid splintering. Steel will undoubtedly last the longest, but a good-quality plastic needle is just as good.

Lengths vary and should be purchased depending on the work you are undertaking. Occasionally, longer needles are necessary, for example, when making a shawl or a blanket where you may have a lot of stitches on your needle, so take this into account when purchasing. The average needle length will vary between 10 in. and 16 in. (25 and 40cm).

Flexible needles are also available and are used for circular knitting, as are double-ended needles, which are used in groups of three or four. Using either of these needle styles will mean you can avoid a seam in your work and work flat circular or tubular pieces of knitting, as well as collars or other styles of neck finishes.

The third needle type is a double-pointed needle (dpn), or cable needle, which can either be straight or have a kink in the middle. It is used as a third needle, along with your standard needles, when cabling or in cross-stitch textured patterns.

A stitch holder is a tool much like a large safety pin, which saves stitches that are to be knitted later. Alternatively, a piece of thread can be passed through the waiting stitches and secured with a double knot. Once you have collected a number of pairs of needles, you will find a knitting gauge very useful. These have a series of holes relating to needle sizes in different countries.

A pair of good-quality embroidery scissors and a selection of darning needles are essential in the knitting tool kit. The scissors need to be kept sharp so that a clean cut is obtained when cutting yarn, and you'll need darning needles with a variety of eye sizes for sewing up different thicknesses.

Knitters' pins have a large, colored end, which keeps the pins from coming free when holding two pieces of work together. A tape measure, notepad, and pencil are the other essentials. A lot of patterns will tell you to knit until work measures a certain length, so the tape is necessary to keep track of this. You will also find that you need to make notes to keep track of stitch numbers, measurements, etc., so a pencil and pad are very useful.

Knitters' graph paper is useful for planning your own patterns and can help you visualize the shape of your written pattern. Ordinary graph paper can be used, but the square format does not relate to the stitch shape, which is oblong, so take this into account.

A crochet hook can be very useful for picking up dropped stitches, and as a general tool it is very practical. Lastly, it is useful to have a selection of buttons and a calculator will be helpful for the tricky math.

Hints and tips

• Have a pencil and paper nearby for making notes. You will find that you often need to count your stitches to check where you are in your work.
• If a pattern asks for a stitch holder and you do not have one, cut a thread of yarn approximately two and a half times the length of your stitches. Thread this through the stitches that you want to save and tie the two ends together with a double reef knot.

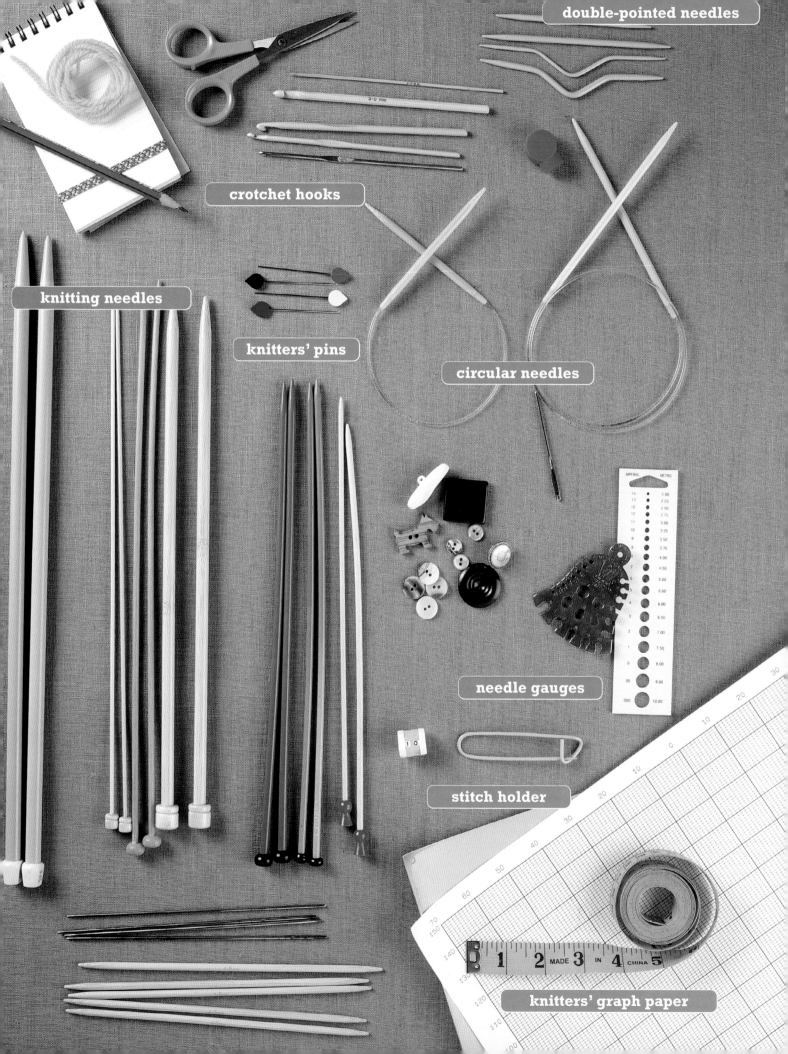

double-pointed needles

crotchet hooks

knitting needles

knitters' pins

circular needles

needle gauges

stitch holder

knitters' graph paper

GAUGE

This term simply refers to the number of stitches and number of rows there are in each square inch of work. If you can achieve the correct gauge, or tension, using stockinette stitch, then you should be able to knit up other stitches correctly.

Gauge, or tension, is one of the most important aspects of knitting. It is a crucial part of interpreting the pattern accurately, enabling you to reproduce the photograph of the pattern and create the item you want. It is affected by needle size, yarn, the stitch pattern, and, lastly, the knitter. A good knitter lets the yarn flow smoothly through the fingers so that even loops are formed on the needles as the stitches are worked.

If your gauge does not match that of the pattern, simply change your needles and try again. Smaller needles will make your work tighter, and larger needles will loosen your work. The larger the needles, the larger your stitches will be, and although most ball bands on knitting yarns recommend a particular needle size, this is an average guide only and may be changed according to the individual's gauge.

Gauge controls the size and shape of your knitting, and every knitter has her own individual gauge. This means that even when two knitters use the same yarn and needles, they will not necessarily produce the same size swatch. For this reason, in order to reproduce a designer's pattern as closely as possible, you should always knit a gauge swatch before starting work. Unless your gauge swatch matches that of the pattern, your work will not be the right size.

Working a gauge swatch
Most patterns give gauge swatches in 4-inch squares. To find a 4-inch gauge, cast on five or so more stitches than the 4-inch measurement requires, and work until the swatch measures about 5 inches square before casting off. Some knitters then prefer to block their swatch and allow it to settle, or to steam the piece, not touching it with the iron but just gushing it with steam, and ease it into shape. This is optional and up to the individual.

Measuring the gauge
To measure the number of stitches, place a ruler or tape measure across the bottom of a row of stitches and mark the beginning and end of your 4-inch width with pins. Count the number of stitches between the pins. To measure the number of rows, measure 4 inches and mark with pins along a vertical column of stitches, being careful to follow the same single column. Count the rows between the pins.

Adjusting the gauge
If your gauge swatch produces too few stitches and rows, make another swatch using smaller needles. If you have too many stitches and rows, then try using larger needles.

Repeat the process until you match the gauge given. Occasionally, however, you may find it impossible to match both stitches and rows. If this happens, match the needles with your stitch gauge, and adjust the number of rows you knit to match the measurements given. Note that if you do change your needles, you must also change any other needles used in the pattern accordingly.

Hints and tips
Blocking the swatch before measuring simply means pinning the piece onto a flat surface, such as a towel or blanket, making sure that the sample is the right way up. Insert the pins vertically all around the swatch, being very careful not to stretch the knitting.

START HERE

These are the basic skills you will acquire. All the information you need to start knitting is here, from how you cast on and off to the basics of knit and purl stitches and shaping your work and, finally, a useful list of hints and tips. Before you even cast on your first row, you need to create a loop for the first stitch, using a slipknot.

Making a slipknot

1   Make a loop by passing the right side of the yarn over the left.

2   With the tail end, pull a second loop through the center of the first loop. Pull the tail end to secure the slipknot.

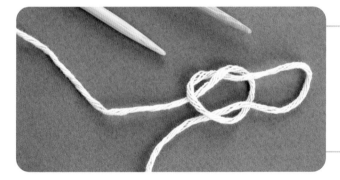

3   Adjust the loop to the correct size for your thumb or knitting needle, depending on which cast-on method you are using (see pages 32–35).

Holding the yarn

It is important to hold your yarn correctly—neither too tight nor too loose. This will come with practice. Some knitters manage to create an even gauge simply by letting the yarn flow across the palm of their hand, others wrap the yarn once around their little finger, and still others combine these two techniques. By passing the yarn under my forefinger, over my middle and ring fingers, and under my little finger, and by bending my fingers loosely into my palm, a gauge is created for my work. Experiment until you find what is comfortable and works for you.

1 Holding the needles in your left hand, if you are right handed, with your palm upper-most, taking the yarn loosely around your little finger.

2 Turn the hand over, wrapping the yarn over your ring finger, under your middle finger.

3 Use your index finger to control the yarn, holding your hand so that this finger can loop over the needles easily. Readjust this movement every now and again to maintain an even tension.

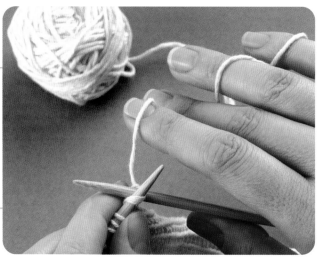

CASTING ON

This is the foundation row of your work. It can be worked in many different styles, but here are the basic methods that you can use. You will soon find your favorite technique, though it is worth trying them all to see which suits you best.

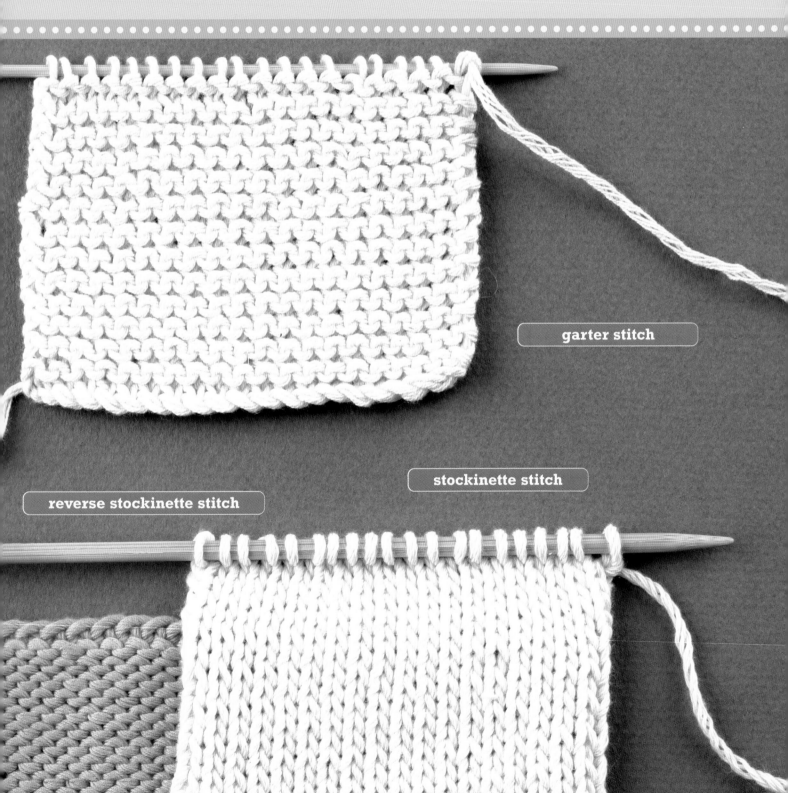

garter stitch

stockinette stitch

reverse stockinette stitch

Casting on with two needles

This method works only if the first row of knitting will be worked into the back of the stitches in the casting-on row. If you do not do this, the edge of your work will be loopy.

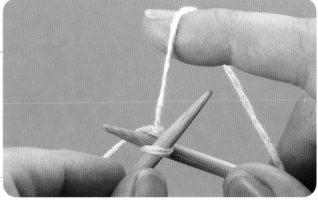

1 Make a slipknot and put it onto the left needle. Put the right needle into the loop so that it passes under the left.

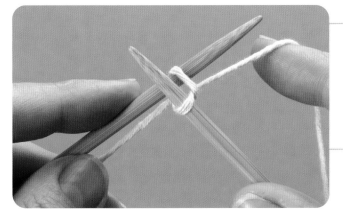

2 Pass the yarn between the needles and take the yarn through the first loop with the right needle.

3 Pass the second loop from the right needle to the left.

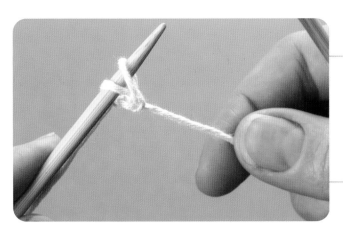

4 Repeat by putting the right needle into the last stitch on the left needle until you have made the required number of stitches.

Casting on: thumb method

Many people prefer to cast on using only one needle and their thumb. The short end of the yarn should be at least three times the length of the final cast-on edge.

1 Make a slipknot with your yarn (see page 30), leaving a tail that is long enough to cast on the number of stitches required. Place the loop on your thumb and insert the point from the right needle into the loop.

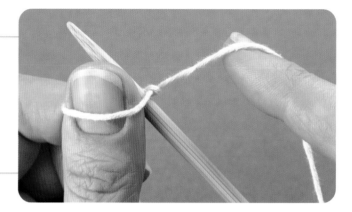

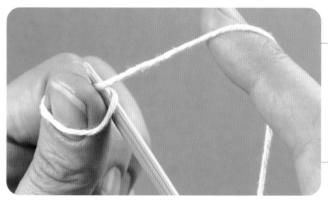

2 With your right hand, wrap the yarn between the point of the needle and the thumb.

3 Draw through the loop on the thumb, then slip the loop over the edge of the needle (thereby knitting the loop). This makes a stitch.

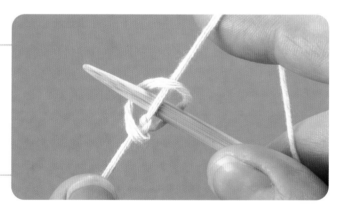

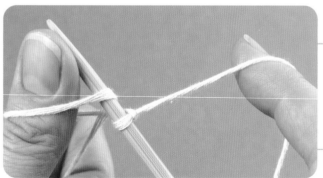

4 Repeat until the required number of stitches is on the needle.

Between-the-stitch method

Also known as the rib, or cable, method, this makes a strong edge and is more decorative than the other casting-on methods, though it may not be as elastic. Follow the method for casting on with two needles for the first two stitches, then make the remaining stitches as follows.

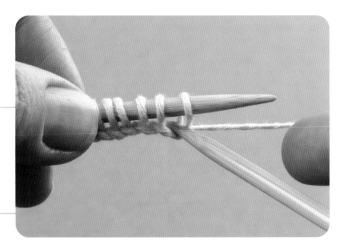

1 Place the right needle between the first and second stitches.

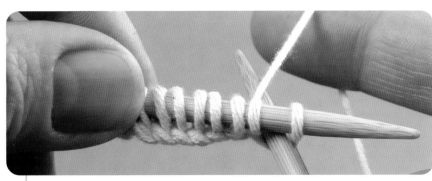

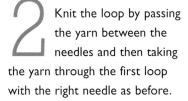

2 Knit the loop by passing the yarn between the needles and then taking the yarn through the first loop with the right needle as before.

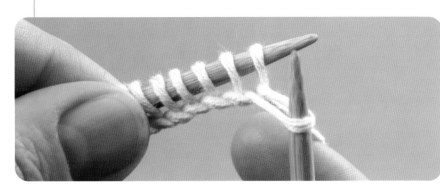

3 Place this new stitch with the other stitches on the left needle. Repeat until the required number of stitches is made.

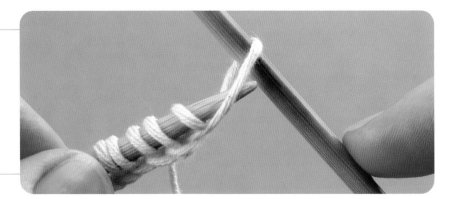

BASIC STITCHES

All knitted fabrics are made up of one or two stitches—knit and purl. Knitting every row in knit stitch produces a fabric called "garter stitch." Working a knit row and then a purl row alternately produces stockinette stitch, which is the method used in most simple patterns. With stockinette stitch, the knit side is the right side, although the purl side may be used as the right side, in which case the fabric is then known as "reversed stockinette stitch."

Knit stitch

Cast on the required number of stitches onto the left needle.

1 Insert the point of the right needle from front to back through the first loop on the left needle.

2 Pass the yarn (which is always at the back of the work for plain knitting) between the two needle points.

3 Draw the loop through to the front of the work. Pull the left needle under the right one, drawing the loop through with it.

4 Maintaining the tension of the yarn with your finger, slip the remaining stitch off the left needle.

5 Your stitch will now be on the right needle. Continue like this to the end of the row. To knit the next row, turn your work around so that the back is facing you and the stitches are on your left needle again. The right needle will now be empty and ready to receive the next row of stitches.

Purl stitch

1 Beginning with the yarn at the front and the wrong side of the work facing you, insert the right needle from back to front into the first stitch on the left needle.

2 Pass the yarn (which for purl is always held in front of your work) over and around the point of the right needle.

3 Draw the loop through.

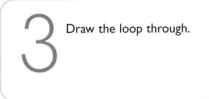

4 Slide the first stitch off the left needle. Continue like this to the end of the row.

Combination stitches

Knit and purl form the basis of all knitting, but it is the combinations of these two stitches that create different stitch textures and patterns. Rib and seed stitch are both simple methods of alternating knit and purl stitches, with endless variations that produce many beautifully textured patterns.

Rib stitch Ribbing consists of alternating knit and purl stitches on the same row to form vertical lines. Rib contracts the fabric but also allows it to be elastic and is often used at the neck and cuff of a garment. The amount of stretch depends on the proportion of knit to purl stitches in each row. For example, a knit 1, purl 1 rib will be the most flexible, whereas a knit 4, purl 1 rib will not contract as much. To get a rib after your first establishing row of knit and purl stitches, work the second row by purling on the knit stitches and knitting on the purl stitches.

Seed stitch Seed stitch, also known as "moss stitch," is a reversible stitch made up of knit and purl stitches that alternate both horizontally and vertically. It forms a flat fabric that spreads more than stockinette stitch and does not curl at the edges. Unlike k1, p1 rib, where on the return rows you knit on the purl stitches and purl on the knit stitches, you continue knitting the knit and purling the purl stitches throughout.

SHAPING

Adding shaping to knitwear by making it wider or narrower is done by increasing or decreasing the number of stitches being worked. The position of any increasing and decreasing will be given in the instructions, and the following notes explain the various ways of doing this.

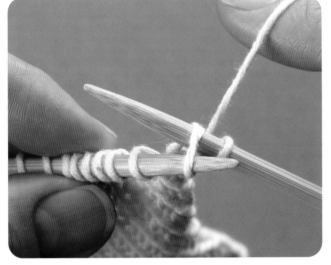

Increasing

This can be done anywhere in a row, but as it is the method used to change the shape of your work, it should always be done where specified in the pattern.

Simple increasing This is where the increase is made on the first or last stitch in a row, and it creates one extra stitch at the increase point. Knit the first stitch, but instead of dropping the stitch off the left needle, place the point of the right needle into the back of the stitch, knit it, and then drop it off the left needle. You now have two stitches on the right needle. Work purl increases in the same way but purlwise.

Although this is a popular method, it has an irregular appearance and looks untidy. It is really suitable only for a seam edge, where it will be hidden when the work is sewn up.

Fully fashioned increasing This is where the increase is made not on the first or last stitch but usually on the third stitch from the edge. It may also be made on the second stitch from the edge or across the work at regular points if you want to widen your work suddenly as a feature.

The mark made when increasing in this way is called a "fashioning mark," and this technique is often used as a design feature, particularly on finer knitwear or when using a smooth yarn such as mercerized cotton. This visible mark on your work is also useful for counting your increases.

1 On a knit row, knit the first two stitches.

2 Then knit the third stitch, but instead of dropping this stitch off the left needle, place the point of the right needle into the back of the stitch, knit this loop, and then drop it off.

Decreasing

This is the shaping that makes your work narrower. You do this by knitting or purling two stitches together to reduce them to one stitch.

Simple decreasing Pass the tip of the right needle through the first two stitches on the left needle and work together, producing one stitch on the right needle. For purl rows, work as above but decrease purlwise.

Fully fashioned decreasing This works two stitches together, but instead of knitting together the end two stitches, work together the second and third or third and fourth stitches to produce a fashioning mark on the right side of your work. This method will produce a slope from left to right. For purl rows, work as above but purlwise.

If the pattern is using decreases on both sides of a garment and uses the marks as a design feature, or if you want your decreases to converge, as in a flared garment, then work as follows.

To get a right-to-left slope on a knit row, at the decrease point, slip the first stitch (pass it to the other needle without knitting it), knit the next stitch, and then pass the slipped stitch over the knitted stitch. To get a right-to-left slope on a purl row, purl the first stitch and then put it back onto the left needle, lift the next stitch over it, and then return it to the right needle.

The fully fashioned decrease method may also be used all across your work. By working together every third and fourth stitch across a row, a rapid decrease is achieved that gives a gathered effect. For an even more gathered appearance, you could repeat on the next row or you could work every first and second stitch together across a row.

BINDING OFF

This is the method by which you finish off your fabric, making sure that your work will not unravel. Always bind or cast off in the appropriate stitch for your work—knitwise on a knit row and purlwise on a purl row. Binding off on a purl row will have less of a tendency to roll, and the edge is less visible from the right side. If binding off a rib, cast off in both knit and purl, following the rib pattern.

Simple binding off

1 On a knit row, knit the first two stitches. On a purl row, purl the first two stitches, then cast off as described above but purling every stitch.

2 With the left needle, lift the first stitch over the second, then knit the second stitch (which is now the first on the needle). Follow this pattern of lifting one stitch over the next, then knitting the next stitch until just one stitch remains. Break off the yarn and pass the tail through the last loop.

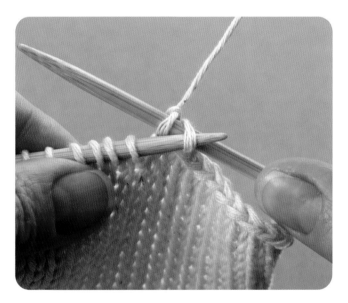

Double binding off

This method spreads out the cast-off row, giving more elasticity to the edge of your work. Knit the first stitch, *then knit into the next stitch, but leave the loop on the left needle. Cast off the stitch on the right needle by lifting the first stitch over the second, then knit again into the old loop (on the left needle) and cast this off. Repeat from * until just one stitch remains.

On a purl row, purl the first stitch, then cast off as described above but purling every stitch. As with simple casting off, you do not need to cast off between every stitch.

Invisible edge casting off

This method is not suitable for seams, but it is very useful for children or other beginners who have simply learned a basic knit stitch, or for gathering up knitting stitches.

Simply thread a length of yarn through all the stitches on each side of the garment and finish off the end by weaving it into your work. This is used on the top of stocking hats to gather them up and secure the stitches at the same time.

Holding the needles

The position of the needles is also crucial to the finished gauge of your knitting. Some knitters hold both needles evenly in front of them, while others secure one needle under the right arm and let the left needle drop diagonally. Yet another style is to secure both needles, one under either arm. Choose the style that makes you feel comfortable, without any strain on your hands, back, or neck, and allows you to work easily.

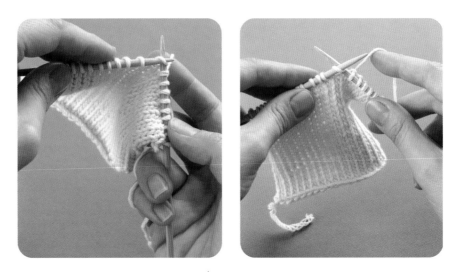

Picking up dropped stitches

With care, you should be able to repair a dropped stitch and correct your work. Try to do this from the right side. To repair a dropped stitch on the wrong side of your work, repair in the same way but with your stitch at the back of your work. If you are repairing a stitch in a patterned piece of work, make sure you knit or purl where appropriate.

❶ Make sure that your stitch is at the front of your work and then use your knitting needle or a crotchet hook to pick up the horizontal threads, pulling each thread through the stitch one at a time until you have picked up all the dropped stitches.
❷ Place the stitch back on your needle.

Hints and tips

• When casting off for children's clothes or other garments where the necks are fitted, it is best to cast off with needles two sizes bigger than the ones you used for knitting.
• Another way of avoiding a tight cast-off edge is to pick up, knit, and then cast off the loop lying between each of the stitches on the needle. This is a slightly less effective method than double casting off.

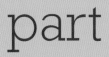

3

BEYOND
THE BASICS

READING PATTERNS

At the beginning of each pattern, the instructions will give you a list of the equipment and materials you need to complete the pattern, including the all-important gauge details and often the finished measurements. The patterns in this book are also graded as to their difficulty from 1, being easy, to 5, the most tricky.

Yarn

The pattern will tell you the required thickness, or ply, of the yarn, for example, fingering weight, sport weight, or worsted weight. Often the pattern will indicate a make and specific color of yarn too, but with experience you will be able to substitute another yarn. As long as it is of the same ply and you make sure your gauge matches the pattern, you should get the same results. This gives you a wider choice of yarns to work with and also the option of working a cotton pattern in wool or vice versa.

Needles

Most patterns will use two sizes of needles, with the smaller one usually being for the ribs or edges of your work. Use the recommended needles unless your gauge doesn't match, in which case change the needles accordingly (see page 29). If you do change needles, remember to make a note on the pattern for future reference. If a cable is being worked, you will need a cable needle as well.

A special knitting bag is useful for keeping everything together. One that can be closed is the most effective, or you could use a craft box with a lid. This keeps your work clean and keeps balls from falling out and unraveling.

Gauge

The combination of yarn and needles will give you the gauge (see page 29). If your gauge does not match, then change your needles and rework your sample until it does. Most patterns will give you the expected finished measurements of your work, most importantly the width and length. These depend on achieving the correct gauge.

Key

If your pattern requires that you follow a graph or involves more than one color (such as for stripes), the key will provide you with the code for each color, usually through a system of letters or numbers representing the different yarns and colors being used. If your pattern uses lots of colors, write the key code on the ball band of each color to save confusion. For complicated intarsia or Fair Isle graphs, the key will use symbols. Each square on the graph represents a stitch, and it will usually have a symbol inside it telling you which color to use. Sometimes the graphs are color-coded instead.

Order of work

Most garment patterns start by knitting the back, and it is advisable to work in the order set out. If it takes a while for your tension to settle down, the back is the least visible place for it to happen.

If a graph is being used, follow it as instructed. Most graphs should be worked from the bottom right-hand corner. The odd rows will be knitted and read from right to left, and the even rows will be purled, reading from left to right. If you read the graph from the opposite way around, any image within the pattern will be reversed. This will not always matter, but it would be crucial if you were working from a graph that knitted a word into the pattern.

Marking progress

When following a graph, it is a good idea to use a ruler as a marker to check your progress on each row, moving it up the graph as you complete each row, or marking each finished row with a pencil. Quite often on a complicated image, no two rows are the same, so it is important to keep track of where you are on your pattern.

Below Gauge swatches worked in different yarns or in the same yarn with different sized needles, will come out differently.

STITCH LIBRARY

The wide variety of materials displayed in the knitting projects of this book are created by only two different stitches—knit and purl. Once these two simple stitches are mastered, the sky is the limit for the texture and variation in your designs. The best way to learn the stitch techniques is to practice, so work through the individual swatches to create your own library of stitches. A guide to abbreviations is on page 181.

❶ Stockinette stitch
R1: k.
R2: p.

❷ Reverse stockinette stitch
R1: p.
R2: k.

❸ Garter stitch
All rows: k.

❹ K2, p2 rib
(multiple of 4 sts)
All rows: k2, p2.

❺ Beaded rib
(multiple of 5 sts plus 2 sts)
R1: *p2, k1, p1, k1, rep from * to last two sts, p2.
R2: k2, *p3, k2, rep from * to end.
Rep R1–2.

❻ Rib and stockinette stitch band
(multiple of 12 sts plus 7 sts)
R1: *p1, k1, p1, k1, p1, k1, p1, k5, rep from * to last 7 sts, then p1, k1, p1, k1, p1, k1, p1.
R2: * k1, p1, k1, p1, k1, p1, k1, p5, rep from * to last 7 sts, then k1, p1, k1, p1, k1, p1, k1.
Rep R1–2.

Knit and purl

❶ Fisherman's rib

(even number of sts)

R1: p.

R2: *p1, k next st in the row below, rep from *
and ending with p2.

Rep R2 only.

❷ Twin rib

(multiple of 6 sts)

R1: *k3, p3, rep from * to end.

R2: *k1, p1, rep from * to end.

Rep R1–2.

❸ Seed stitch

(multiple of 2 sts)

R1: k1, p1.

R2: p1, k1.

❹ Double seed stitch

(multiple of 4 sts)

R1 and 2: *k2, p2, rep from * to end.

R3 and 4: *p2, k2, rep from * to end.

Rep R3–4.

❺ Stripe seed stitch

(multiple of 11 sts plus 5 sts)

R1: k5 *(k1, p1) three times, k5, rep from * to end.

R2: *p5 (p1, k1) three times, rep from * to last 5
sts, p5.

Rep R1–2.

❻ Roman stitch

(even number of sts)

R1 and 3: k.

R2 and 4: p.

R5: *k1, p1, rep from * to end.

R6: *p1, k1, rep from * to end.

Rep R1–6.

Textures with knit and purl

❶ K1, p1 rib
(multiple of 2 sts)

All rows: k1, p1.

❷ Reverse ridge
(any number of sts)

R1 (RS): k.
R2: p.
R3–8: k.
Rep R1–8.

❸ Garter stitch zigzag
(multiple of 6 sts)

R1 (WS) and all WS rows: p.
R2: *k3, p3, rep from * to end.
R4: p1, *k3, p3, rep from * ending last rep with p2 instead of p3.
R6: p2, *k3, p3, rep from * ending last rep with p1 instead of p3.
R8: *p3, k3, rep from * to end.
R10: p2, *k3, p3, rep from * ending last rep with p1 instead of p3.
R12: p1, *k3, p3, rep from * ending last rep with p2 instead of p3.
Rep R1–12.

❹ Garter stitch ridge
(any number of sts)

R1 and 3: k.
R2: p.
R4: k (p side of work).
Rep R1–4.

❺ Rectangular check
(multiple of 6 sts)

R1 and alternate rows: k.
R2, 4, 6, 8, 10, 12: *k3, p3, rep from * to end.
R14, 16, 18, 20, 22, 24: *p3, k3, rep from * to end.

❻ Variation on normal cable
(multiples of 10 sts)

R1 and 3(WS): k2, p6, k2
R2: p2, k6, p2.
R4: p2, sl next 3 sts onto dpn and cable back, k3, then k3 from dpn, p2.
Rep R1–4.
R5, 7, 9, 11, 13, 15, 17 (WS): k2, p6, k2.
R6, 8, 12, 14, 16, 18: p2, k6, p2.
R10: p2, sl next 3 sts onto dpn and cable back, k3, then k3 from dpn, p2.
Rep R1–18.

1

2

3

4

5

6

Cables

A very small collection of cables is included here to get you started. In addition, I have included a cable and rope panel and a chain and seed-stitch panel as examples of how a cable can also combine texture.

❶ Plait cable panel of 13 sts

R1 and 5 (RS): p2, k9, p2.
R2, 4, 6, 8: k2, p9, k2.
R3: p2, sl 3 sts onto dpn and cable front, k3, then k3 from dpn, k3, p2.
R7: p2, k3, sl 3 sts onto dpn and cable back, k3, then k3 from dpn, p2.
Rep R1–8.

❸ Panel of 8 sts

R1 and 3(WS): k2, p6, k2
R2: p2, k6, p2.
R4: p2, sl next 3 sts onto dpn and cable back, k3, then k3 from dpn, p2.
Rep R1–4.
R5, 7, 9, 11, 13, 15, 17 (WS): k2, p6, k2.
R6, 8, 12, 14, 16, 18: p2, k6, p2.
R10: p2, sl next 3 sts onto dpn and cable back, k3, then k3 from dpn, p2. Rep R1–18.

❺ Cable and rope panel

R1: p7, sl 3 sts onto dpn and cable front, k3, then k3 from dpn, p7.
R2: k7, p6, k7.
R3: p7, k6, p7.
R4: p5, k2, p6, k2, p5.
R5: k5, p2, k6, p2, k5.
R6: p5, k2, p6, k2, p5.

❷ Basic cable panel of 8 sts

(cable 4 sts)
R1 and 3 (WS): k2, p4, k2.
R2: p2, k4, p2.
R4: p2, sl next 2 sts onto dpn and cable back, k2, then k2 from dpn, p2. Rep R1–4.

❹ Basic cable panel of 10 sts

(cable 6 sts)
R1, 3, 5 (WS): k2, p6, k2.
R2 and 4: p2, k6, p2.
R6: p2, sl next 3 sts onto dpn and cable back, k3, then k3 from dpn, p2. Rep R1–6.

❻ Chain and seed-stitch cable

R1 and 3: p3, k3, work 6 sts in seed st, k3, p3.
R2 and 4: k3, p3, work 6 sts in seed st, p3, k3.
R5: p3, sl 3 sts onto dpn and cable back, work next 3 sts in seed st, k3 from dpn, sl 3 sts onto dpn and cable front, k3, work next 3 sts in seed st, p3.
R6, 8, 10, 12, 14: k3, work 3 sts in seed st, p6, work 3 sts in seed st, k3.
R7, 9, 11, 13: p3, work 3 sts in seed st, k6, work 3 sts in seed st, p3.
R15: p3, sl 3 sts onto dpn and cable front, k3, work 3 sts from dpn in seed st, slip 3 sts onto dpn and cable back, work next 3 sts in seed st, k3 from dpn, p3.
R16, 18, 20, 22, 24, 26, 28: k3, p3, work 6 sts in seed st, p3, k3.
R17, 19, 21, 23, 25, 27: p3, k3, work 6 sts in seed st, k3, p3. Rep R5–R28.

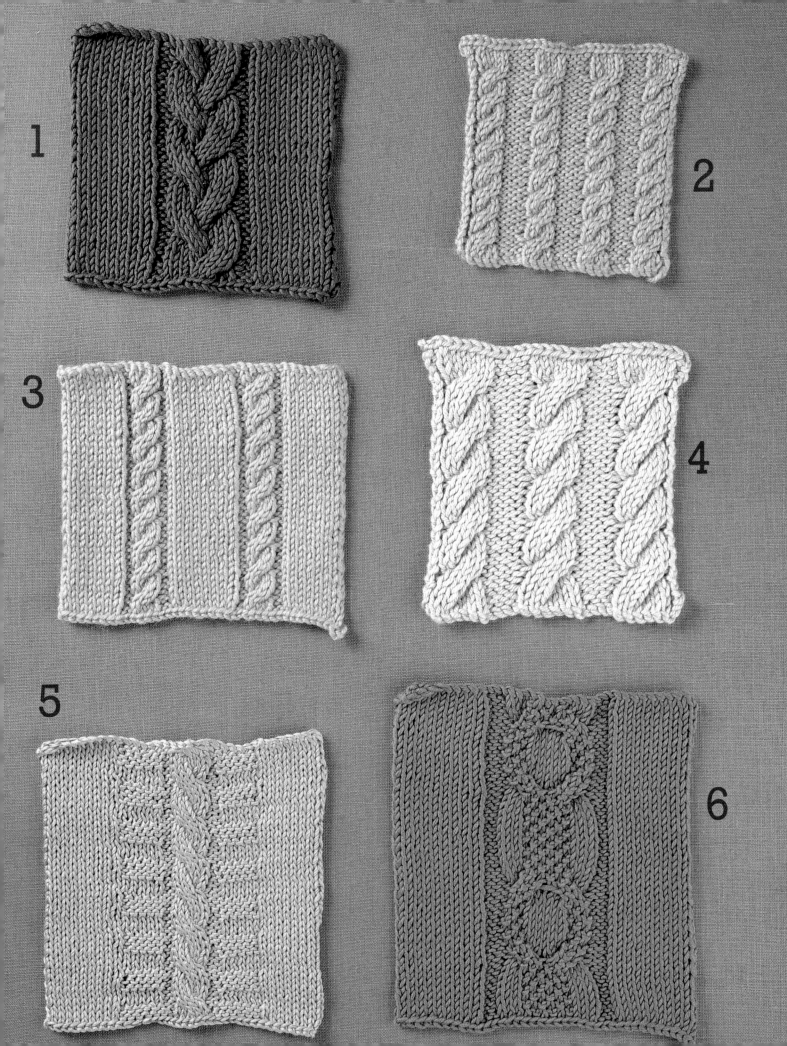

Color and lace stitches

❶ Two-color tweed stitch
(multiple of 3 sts)
R1: MC, *sl 1 pwise, k2, rep from * to end
R2: MC, k.
R3: CC, *k2, sl 1 pwise, rep from * to end.
R4: CC, k.
Rep R1–4.

❷ Fan stitch
(multiple of 18 sts)
R1 (RS): k.
R2: p.
R3: *(k2tog) 3 times, (yon, k1) 6 times, (k2tog) 3 times, rep from * to end.
R4: k.
Rep R1–4.

❸ Woven stripe
(two colors—MC and CC; odd number of sts)
R1 and 11 (RS): MC, k.
R2 and 12: MC, p.
R3 and 13: CC, k1, *sl 1, wyif, k1, rep from * to end.
R4 and 14: CC, p.
R5 and 15: MC, k2, *sl 1, wyif, k1, rep from * to end.
R6 and 16: MC, p.
R7 and 17: MC, k.
R8 and 18: MC, p.
R9 and 19: CC, k1, *sl 1, wyif, k1, rep from * to end.
R10 and 20: CC, p.
Rep R1–20.

❹ Lace stitch
(multiple of 10 sts plus 1 st)
R1 (RS): k1, *yfd, k3, k3tog, k3, yfd, k1, rep from * to end.
R2: k.
Rep R1–2.

❺ Eyelet lace (uneven number of sts)
R1: k. R2: p.
R3 and 4: k.
R5: *k2tog, yon, rep from * to last st, k1.
R6: k.
Rep R1–6.

❻ Small leaf lace
(multiple of 6 sts plus 3 sts)
R1: k1, p2, k3, *p3, k3, rep from * to last 3 sts, p2, k1.
R2 and 4: k3, *p3, k3, rep from * to end.
R3: k1, p2, *yon, k3tog, yrn, p3, rep from * to last 6 sts, yon, k3tog, yrn, p2, k1.
Rep R1–4.

1

2

3

4

5

6

Color and lace stitches

❶ Very simple lace stitch

(multiple of 8 sts)

R1 (RS): k.

R2 and all alternate rows (WS): p.

R3: *k6, yon, k2tog, rep from * to end.

R5: k.

R7: k2, *yon, k2tog, k6, rep from * ending last rep with k4.

R8: p.

Rep R1–8.

❸ Purse stitch and chevron lace

(multiple of 7 sts)

R1: *k2, sl 1, k2tog, psso, k2, yon, rep from * to end.

R2: *p6, yrn, rep from * to end.

Rep R1–2.

❺ Poncho stripe (three colors—MC, CC1, and CC2; multiple of 4 plus 3 sts)

R1 (RS): MC, k3, *wyib, sl 1, k3, rep from * to end.

R2 (WS): MC, k3, *wyif, sl 1, yb, k3, repeat from * to end.

R3: CC1, k1, *wyib, sl 1, k3, rep from * to last 2 sts, yb, sl 1, k1.

R4: CC1, k1, *wyif, sl 1, yb, k3, rep from * to last 2 sts, wyif, sl 1, yb, k1.

R5: CC2, work as R1.

R6: CC2, work as R3.

Rep R1–6, changing colors every other row.

Rep R1–8.

> Edgings can be made wider or narrower by increasing or decreasing the number of stitches at the beginning. Shallower scallops can be made by increasing and decreasing every alternate row.

❷ Alternative poncho stripe

(with five colors—multiple of 4 plus 3 sts)

❹ Fringe

Using a double end of yarn, cast on 13 sts.

R1: k2, yon, k2tog, k1, yon, k2tog, k6.

R2: p5, k2 (yon, k2tog, k1) twice.

Rep R1–2 until the fringe measures the required length, ending with a R2.

Next row: sl 1, then bind off next 7 sts. Draw yarn through and finish. Drop rem 5 sts off needle and unravel them back to beg of work, making fringe loops.

❻ Turret edging

Cast on 6 sts.

R1, 2, 3: k.

R4: cast on 3 sts, k.

R5, 6, 7: k.

R8: cast on 3 sts, k.

R9, 11, 13, 14, 15: k.

R10 and 12: p.

R16: bind-off 3 sts, k to end.

R17, 18, 19: k.

R20: bind-off 3 sts, k to end.

Rep R1–20.

❼ Garter scallop edging

Cast on 7 sts, k 1 row.

R1: k5, inc in next st (by working into front, then back of stitch), k1.

R2: k1, inc in next st, k6.

R3: k7, inc in next st, k1.

R4: k1, inc in next st, k8.

R5: k9, inc in next st, k1.

R6: k1, inc in next st, k10.

R7: k11, inc in next st, k1.

R8: k1, inc in next st, k12.

R9: k12, k2tog, k1.

R10: k1, k2tog, k11.

R11: k10, k2tog, k1.

R12: k1, k2tog, k9.

R13: k8, k2tog, k1.

R14: k1, k2tog, k7.

R15: k6, k2tog, k1.

R16: k1, k2tog, k5.

Rep R1–16.

Decorative textures

❶ Quaker ridge
(any number of sts)
R1, 3, 5, 6, 7, 9, 11, 12, 14 (RS): k.
R2, 4, 8, 10, 13: p.
Rep R1–14.

❸ Chevron pattern
(multiple of 8 sts plus 1 st)
R1 and 10: k1, *p7, k1, rep from * to end.
R2 and 9: p1, *k7, p1, rep from * to end.
R3 and 12: k2, *p5, k3, rep from * ending with p5, k2.
R4 and 11: p2, *k5, p3, rep from * ending with k5, p2.
R5 and 14: k3, *p3, k5, rep from * ending with p3, k3.
R6 and 13: p3, *k3, p5, rep from * ending with k3, p3.
R7 and 16: k4, *p1, k7, rep from * ending with p1, k4
R8 and 15: p4, *k1, p7, rep from * ending with k1, p4.
Rep R1–16.

❷ Diamond brocade
(multiple of 8 sts plus 1 st)
R1 (RS): k4, *p1, k7, rep from * ending last rep p1, k4.
R2 and 8: p3, *k1, p1, k1, p5, rep from * ending last rep p3.
R3 and 7: k2, *p1, k3, rep from * ending last rep k2.
R4 and 6: p1, *k1, p5, k1, p1, rep from * to end.
R5: *p1, k7, rep from * ending last rep p1.
Rep R1–8.

❹ Embossed leaf pattern
(multiple of 10 sts)
R1, 3, 4, 16: p.
R2 and 10: k.
R5: *p5, k5, rep from * to end.
R6 and 11: *k1, p5, k4, rep from * to end.
R7 and 12: *p3, k5, p2, rep from * to end.
R8 and 13: *k3, p5, k2, rep from * to end.
R9 and 14: *p1, k5, p4, rep from * to end.
R15: *k5, p5, rep from * to end.
Rep R1–16.

Checks and diamonds

❶ Cross and diamond repeat

This is the same as the cross and diamond border on the right, but repeating R3–12.

❸ Vandyke check pattern

(multiple of 8 sts)

R1 and 7: k.
R2, 8, 9, 10, 11, 17: *k4, p4, rep from * to end.
R3: p1, *k4, p4, rep from * ending last rep p3 instead of p4.
R4: k2, *p4, k4, rep from * ending last rep k2 instead of k4.
R5: p3, *k4, p4, rep from * ending last rep p1 instead of p4.
R6 and 13: *p4, k4, rep from * to end.
R12 and 18: p.
R14: k1, *p4, k4, rep from * ending last rep k3 instead of k4.
R15: p2, *k4, p4, rep from * ending last rep p2 instead of p4.
R16: k3, *p4, k4, rep from * ending last rep k1 instead of k4.
R19, 20, 21, 22: *p4, k4, rep from * to end.
Rep R1–22.

❷ Cross and diamond border

(multiple of 16 sts plus 1 st)

R1 (RS): k.
R2 and 14: k.
R3 and 13: k1, *k4, (p1, k5) twice, rep from * to end.
R4 and 12: p1, *(p3, k1) 3 times, p4, rep from * to end.
R5 and 11: k1, *k2, p1, k3, p1, k1, (p1, k3) twice, rep from * to end.
R6 and 10: p1, *p1, k1, (p3, k1) 3 times, p2, rep from * to end of row.
R7 and 9: k1, *p1, k3, p1, k5, p1, k3, p1, k1, rep from * to end.
R8: k1, *p3, k1, p7, k1, p3, k1, rep from * to end.
This makes a border 14 rows high. If you want horizontal bands of this pattern, rep R3–12.

❹ Simple drop stitch

R1: k, winding yrn 3 times.
R2: p, letting the extra 2 loops drop to form an elongated row.
Work a st st band between the drop st row as desired.
Variations on this stitch could be to work garter stitch or seed stitch between the drop stitch rows.

❺ Caterpillar stitch

(multiple of 10 sts)

R1: *k4, p6, rep from * to end.
R2, 4, 6, 8: p.
R3: k.
R5: *p5, k4, p1, rep from * to end.
R7: k. Rep R1–8.

❻ Tile stitch

(multiple of 5 sts)

R1, 3, 5, 7: k.
R2, 4, 6: *p4, k1, rep from * to end.
R8: k.
Rep R1–8.

1

2

3

4

5

6

MANAGING COLOR

The art of successfully working with more than one color is to keep all those balls and bobbins under control. Take a firm hand with your yarn, otherwise you will end up with a mess—or worse, with holes where the different yarns meet.

Joining in a new color

When joining in a new color or fresh ball of yarn, tie the ends together to prevent unraveling and to keep a hole from being produced. Leave long ends so that they are useful for sewing up seams during finishing.

Placing a stitch marker

Sometimes it is necessary to mark your work so that you can keep track of shaping, color changes, or row counts. To place a stitch marker, wrap a contrast-colored piece of yarn around the stitch you wish to mark and tie it in a double knot.

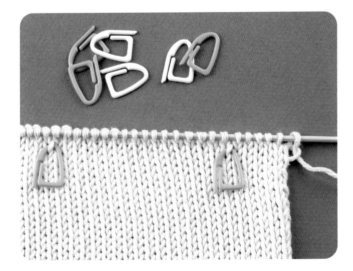

Alternatively, use plastic markers sold in craft or yarn stores.

Intarsia knitting

There are two ways of using more than two colors in a row. The most popular is Fair Isle, which is where the yarn not being worked is woven or stranded across the back of the work and picked up where it is needed.

However, some patterns, and particularly one-off images, use color in large blocks. To work these, you need a method that keeps the gauge even and your work flat. This method is known as "intarsia," or color blocking. Without the use of intarsia, you would have to weave yarn across the back of large areas of single colors, which would not only look very untidy but would also badly distort the image and make the work too thick. Also, it is very difficult to keep an even gauge if a single thread is constantly weaving across the back of your work.

When you are working an image from a graph, use intarsia for any area of one color that is more than five stitches across. Also, make sure you check your progress by marking the graph as you go (see page 47).

You can work intarsia in both knit and purl. At the appropriate point, add a second color by twisting the two yarns around each other on the wrong side where they meet, thus avoiding gaps in the work. Repeat this process on each row where colors meet. When the work is finished, you will need to weave the ends vertically down the loops where the colors meet. Never weave the ends horizontally into the work, as this will show on the right side and may also unravel, appearing on the right side.

Fair Isle

Fair Isle is usually worked from a chart. Each square represents a stitch and each row of squares, a knitted row. Either colors or symbols will correspond with the different colors being knitted. Work the chart from bottom to top in stockinette stitch, usually reading each odd-numbered (knit; RS) row from right to left and each even-numbered (purl; WS) row from left to right.

When knitting Fair Isle, you will have two colors on each row, and the colors not being used must be woven or stranded across the back of the work. There are two main techniques used for this: stranding and weaving in.

Stranding This where the yarn is left loose across the back of the work, but will never pass more than four or five stitches before being picked up and used again.

Weaving in Here the yarn not being knitted is woven over and under the color in use. The color not in use is passed over the color in use when knitting one stitch and under the color in use on the following stitch. Stranding (see below) is the traditional method used in the Shetland Islands, and it keeps a softer, more pliable feel to the work. However, these strands mustn't be pulled too tightly, as they can greatly distort the garment if they're not even.

ADDING EMBROIDERY

Adding color and design to your work does not have to include difficult knitting techniques. These designs can be an afterthought that will enhance your creations.

Blanket stitch

1 Working from right to left and with the edge of the fabric at the top, bring a darning needle threaded with yarn through at the bottom of the edging.

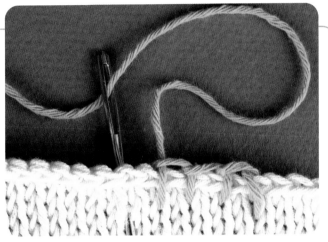

2 Hold the thread down and insert the needle to the right, by the top edge of the work, taking a straight stitch that emerges inside the loop. Pull the needle through until the thread forms a horizontal bar and continue working to the right.

Chain stitch

Draw a needle through the fabric from back to front, then reinsert the needle just to the right of where it came through, holding some of the thread down to create a small loop. Take a stitch of the required length, making sure the needle passes up through the loop to form the first chain link. Repeat, shaping the chain stitches around your work as required.

Swiss darning

This embroidery stitch done onto the top of stockinette stitch follows the line of the stitch, superimposing a contrast color onto the front surface of your work to create a pattern that looks as if it's been knitted in.

With a darning needle and contrast thread, trace the pattern of the stitch, beginning at the bottom edge of the stitch. From behind, pass it through the center of the stitch and up and under the two threads of the stitch above, then back into the space where the thread first appeared. Repeat, covering as many stitches as required.

You could also embroider a pattern in this stitch using different colors by working it out on graph paper first.

BUTTONHOLES

It is important to place buttonholes in the correct place, which is two or three stitches in from the edge of the work. It is often worth oversewing your buttonhole to give it a firm edge, since with time the wear on the threads on either side of the hole may cause the yarn to break and unravel. To do this, simply work an overstitch or small blanket stitch around each buttonhole.

There are three different styles of buttonhole: eyelet, horizontal, and vertical.

Vertical This buttonhole style is needed only where the strain on the button is up or down. It is very simple to do. Simply divide your work in two to make a vertical slit. At the point where the buttonhole begins, keep the remaining stitches on a stitch holder and continue knitting the stitches on your needle until the buttonhole measures the required length. Then keep these stitches on a stitch holder and repeat on the opposite side. When the work is of the same length, continue on all the stitches together, so completing the buttonhole (see right).

Horizontal

This is the most common buttonhole to work. It is used where the strain is from side to side, as on a cardigan button band. This method can be used to make a buttonhole for any size button.

1 At the required position and starting on a knit row, cast off the number of stitches required for the size of your button. On the return row, cast on over the cast-off stitches using the thumb method (see page 34) and work to the end of the row.

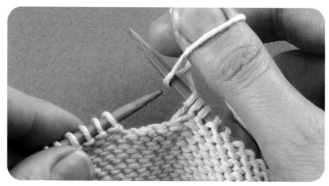

2 On the following rows, knit or purl the stitches, so that there are the number of stitches in the row is restored.

Eyelet

This buttonhole is suitable for fine knitwear or baby wear and can also be used as a method for threading ribbon.

1 Working on a knit row, when you come to the place to make the eyelet buttonhole, put the yarn forward around the needle.

2 K2tog, then In the next row, the made stitch is purled in the usual way and small hole is formed.

Sewing on a button

Where possible, use strands of yarn from your work to attach the button. When you have sewn the button on firmly, create a shank by wrapping the yarn around the base of the button, thereby strengthening the threads that join the button to the garment.

Making a button loop

On the opposite side to your button, make a loop with the same yarn that will fit over the button. Anchor the yarn at either end, and strengthen this loop by working blanket stitch along its length. Fasten off the yarn at the other end, working the end along the edge before cutting off.

FINISHING

Different weights of garment will require different preparations before being sewn up. Generally, the heavier the fabric, the less need there is for pulling the individual pieces into place using blocking or steaming before sewing up.

Blocking

This simply means pinning out the knitted pieces on a flat surface (usually a blanket or towel covered in cotton) and making sure the measurements are correct. It also enables you to pull all the stitches into place.

Pin all around the work, sticking the pins in vertically through the garment at 3- to 4-inch intervals into the soft surface below. Do not block any ribbing that is on a garment—this should be left loose.

Steaming

Never iron your work directly, as it may burn or distort it and it is hard to get a garment back to the correct shape once it has been damaged.

As an alternative to pressing pieces before sewing them up, you can sew them up first and then steam the garment with strong gusts of steam from an iron.

Using a damp cloth with a hot, dry iron instead of using a steam iron is also very effective, but you must keep the cloth damp at all times. Have a bowl of water beside you as you iron, so that you can dip the cloth into it to redampen it. Place the damp cloth onto the garment and press with the hot iron.

Sewing up

Having checked your pieces and prepared them (if necessary), you are now ready for the final stages of tidying up any ends and sewing the seams. If you have used contrast colors and the yarn has met midrow, weave the ends along the meeting point of the two colors. Never sew in ends across your work, as they will show and tend to pop through to the right side.

Backstitch

Use backstitch for the shoulder seams. This is a quick and firm stitch, which most people know how to do. It is done with right sides together. Working from left to right, bring the needle to the front and take it back in two stitches later. Go back on stitch and perform the same movement again—moving two steps forward and one step back.

Hints and tips

Sew your seams in the correct order to avoid confusion. ❶ Sew the shoulder seams. ❷ Set in the sleeves matching the center to the shoulder seam. ❸ Side and sleeve seams should be sewn all together to avoid bulkiness in the arm. ❹ Collars or neckbands. ❺ Buttonbands. ❻ Pockets, patch or invisible. ❼ Hems (not usually necessary where ribbing has been used as an edge).

Mattress stitch

The best way to sew side seams together is using mattress stitch. It creates a wonderful flat seam that is strong and versatile and quick to do. If done well, it should be invisible.

1 Arrange the two pieces to be joined side by side, with their right sides facing you. Insert a threaded darning needle into the edge of one of the pieces from front to back, following a vertical line between the end and second to end stitch. Bring the needle up after two rows then pass the needle to the opposite side and repeat.

2 Continue in this way, pulling the edges together and being careful to follow the same vertical line.

Edge-to-edge stitch

There is also an edge-to-edge method that will form an almost invisible seam and will prevent any bulk or hardness to shoulder seam–type edges. With right sides facing you, insert a threaded darning needle from below into the end stitch. Pull the thread through, then insert the needle into the matching stitch on the opposite piece and pass through two loops, coming out onto the right side. Insert the needle back into the original stitch where the thread first appeared. This has the effect of a stitch that is sewn, not knitted.

Finishing the seams

Once the seams have been sewn, sew in any loose yarn ends by weaving them vertically into the seams.

part

4

THE PROJECTS

Home

The projects in this section are designed for you to produce stunning interior accessories for the home. The cushion selection incorporates a range of knitting skills, and the charming simplicity of the coat hangers will enable even the novice knitter to make a beautiful item of which to be proud. The Navajo throw would be perfect in any setting.

PATTERN SPECIFICATIONS:

- Yarn: bulky wool 6 x 2-oz. balls MC; 5 x 2-oz. balls CC1 and CC2
- Needles: #10 (6 mm)

Gauge: 15 sts/20 rows = 4 in. over stocking stitch

Measurements: 27 x 27 in.

Grade: 3

Key:
MC = blue
CC1 = turquoise
CC2 = cream

Squares cushion cover

Front

With MC, cast on 102 sts and follow graph beg bottom right corner. At R21, begin intarsia square using CC1 and MC. Follow graph to end. Bind off.

Back

With MC, cast on 102 sts and work stripes as follows:
12 rows MC
11 rows CC1
2 rows CC2
2 rows CC1
2 rows MC
12 rows CC2
6 rows CC1
6 rows MC
6 rows CC1
10 rows CC2

12 rows MC
8 rows CC2
22 rows CC1
2 rows CC2
4 rows MC
4 rows CC1
2 rows CC2
15 rows MC
Bind off.

Making up

Weave in ends. With RS to RS, sew three sides of cushion, then turn cushion cover RS out. Place 27 x 27-in. cushion pad inside and pin seam. Sew from RS with neat catch st.

Variation

Knit back in same pattern as front or plain st st.

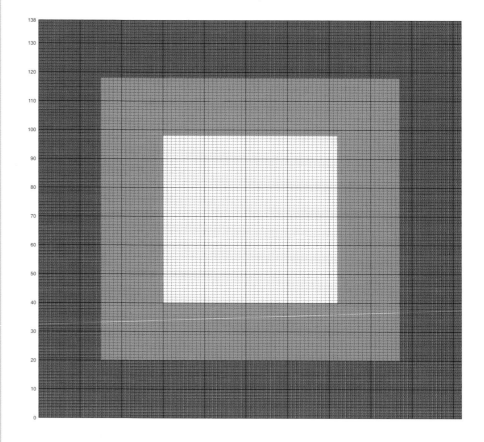

Cross cushion cover

Front and back

With MC, cast on 102 sts and follow graph, beg bottom right corner. At R21 begin intarsia cross using CC and MC. Follow graph to end. Then continue in MC for 138 more rows and bind off. This knits cushion back and front all in one.

Making up

Weave in ends. With RS to RS, fold cushion cover in half and sew side seams. Place 27 x 27-in. cushion pad inside and pin seam. Sew from RS with mattress st or any neat, flat, catch stitch.

Variations

Knit back in same pattern as front or in stripes (as on squares cushion). Work front only and cut a fabric back for cushion cover.

PATTERN SPECIFICATIONS:

- Yarn: bulky wool 10 x 2-oz. balls MC; 3 x 2-oz. balls CC
- Needles: #10 (6 mm)

Gauge: 15 sts/20 rows = 4 in.

Measurements: 27 x 27 in.

Grade: 2

Key:
MC = stone
CC = brown

Navajo throw

With CC1, cast on 120 sts.
R1: *k1, p1, rep from * to end. Change to MC.
R2: *p1, k1, rep from * to end.
These 2 rows form seed st pattern.
Cont in seed st for 4¾ in. more, then:
Change to CC2, work 10 rows.
Change to CC3, work 10 rows.
Change to CC4, work 10 rows.
Change to MC, work 12 rows.
Change to CC5, work 10 rows.
Change to CC6, work 10 rows.
Change to CC7, work 10 rows.
Change to MC, work for 32 in.
Change to CC7, work 10 rows.
Change to CC6, work 10 rows.
Change to CC5, work 10 rows.
Change to MC, work 12 rows.
Change to CC4, work 10 rows.
Change to CC3, work 10 rows.
Change to CC2, work 10 rows.
Change to MC, work for 4¾ in.
Work 1 row more.
Change to CC1, work 1 row, and then bind off.

PATTERN SPECIFICATIONS:

- Yarn: bulky 17 x 2-oz. balls MC; 1 x 2-oz. ball CC1–7.
- Needles: #10 (6 mm)

Gauge: 15 sts/20 rows = 4 in.

Measurements: 34 x 70 in. approx. (Due to the size and weight of this throw and the nature of seed st, the finished size may vary.)

Grade: 2

Key:
MC = sand
CC1 = ocher
CC2 = wine
CC3 = red
CC4 = pink
CC5 = olive
CC6 = lime
CC7 = sage

Note:
These are the quantities used for this sample. However, due to nature of seed st, if your knitting is loose, you may find you need just over 2 oz. of CC2–4 and 5–7.

PATTERN SPECIFICATIONS:

- Yarn: sport weight cotton 6 x 2-oz. balls
- Needles: #6 (4 mm) and dpn

Gauge: 18 sts/34 rows = 4 in. in seed st

Measurements: 16 x 16 in.

Grade: 3

Cable and seed-stitch cushion

Seed st: even no of sts.
R1: *k1, p1, rep from * to end.
R2: *p1, k1, rep from * to end.
Cast on 86 sts.
R1, 3, 5 (WS): k1, p1, k1, p1, k1, p1, k1, p1, k1, p1, k6, p6, k6, *p1, k1, rep from * 14 times more, k6, p6, k6, then p1, k1 to end.
R2 and 6: k1, p1, k1, p1, k1, p1, k1, p1, k1, p7, k6, p6, *k1, p1, rep from * 14 times more, p6, k6, p7, then k1, p1 to end.
R4: k1, p1, k1, p1, k1, p1, k1, p1, k1, p7, sl next 3 sts to dpn and hold at back of work, k3, k3 from dpn, p6, *k1, p1, rep from * 14 times, p6, sl next 3 sts

onto dpn and cable back, k3, k3 from dpn, p6, then p1, k1 to end.
These 6 rows form the pattern.
Rep R1–6 until work measures 32 in. (do not end on a cable row), then bind off.

Making up

Steam work into shape or press with a damp cloth.
Fold cushion in half, RS to RS, matching bind off to bind off edge. Sew side seams. Turn cover to RS and place around 16 x 16-in. cushion pad. Sew top, catching each side together to form a flat seam.

Cables

A cable pattern, which is usually worked on the knit row, gives an embossed effect to your knitting. There are numerous variations on cable patterns, some of which look very complicated but are worth attempting for their stunning results.

In addition to your yarn and knitting needles, you will need a double-pointed needle (dpn) to work a cable. The dpn holds the stitches so that the twist in your work can be made. Slip the first group of stitches in your cable onto the dpn, then place this either at the front or back of your work. Knit the number of stitches specified in the pattern, followed by the stitches from the dpn.

Holding the stitches on the dpn at

the back of your work produces a cable that twists to the right, while holding the stitches on the dpn at the front of your work gives a cable that twists to the left. If you are knitting two cables on either side of a textured panel, making one cable twist to the right and the other to the left will give your work balance.

Most basic cables are crossed after you have worked the same number of rows as there are stitches in the width of the cable, but by crossing the stitches after fewer rows have been worked, a more corded effect is achieved. Experiment with this once you have grasped the basic method. To cross a four-stitch cable, follow the steps opposite.

① Work (following your pattern) to the row where you want to make the cable cross, then work to the four stitches of cable. There will usually be at least one purl stitch on either side of a cable, which helps the cable stand out. Put the next two stitches onto the dpn.

② Knit the next two stitches, then knit the two stitches from the dpn.

③ Continue working in the pattern to the end.

Caterpillar cushion

With 4 mm needles, cast on 90/110 sts,

R1: *k4, p6, rep from * to end of row.

R2: p4, p6, p8

R3: knit

R5: *p5, k4, p1, rep from * to end of row.

R7: knit.

Rep rows 1–7 until work measures 34½ in./42½ in. ending on a purl row where the next row is not r1 or r5 of pattern.

Make buttonholes.

Next row: k12/8, *cast off 4 sts, k14, rep from * 3/4 times more, cast off 4 sts, k12/8.

Next row: p12/8, cast on 4 sts, *p14, cast on 4 sts, rep from * 3/4 times more, p12/8.

Work 2 cm more in pattern. Bind off.

Make up

Fold both ends of work into center, RS to RS, overlapping ends by 4 in. with button band on inside (RS).

Cushion should now measure 15¾ in./19¾ in. square. Pin side seams and sew with firm back stitch.

Fold to right side, press, and then sew on buttons.

PATTERN SPECIFICATIONS:

- Yarn: DK cotton 10 x 2 oz. balls
- Needles: #6 (4 mm)
- 5 (6) buttons
- 1 cushion pad in appropriate size

Gauge: 20–22 sts and 30 rows = 4 in.

Measurements: 15¾ in. x 15¾ in. cushion; for 19¾ in. x 19¾ in. cushion, use the second measurements

Grade: 2

Coat hanger cover

Hanger cover

Cast on 17 sts and work in garter st (knit every row) until strip measures length of coat hanger when slightly stretched. Bind off.

Hook cover

To cover a 5½-in. hook, cast on 38 sts (measure your hanger hook and adjust accordingly), then work 4 rows garter st. Bind off.

Making up

To cover hanger, find center of work in both length and width and slip this point over hanger hook. Stitch bottom and both ends together with a neat catch stitch.

To cover hook, fold strip around hook and sew edges together so that hook is covered. Attach to hanger cover with catch stitch to keep hook cover slipping off.

Lavender bag

Cast on 22 sts and work in garter st for 4 rows, then work in st st for 8 in., work 4 rows in garter st, and bind off.

With a contrast thread, embroider a chain stitch motif such as a heart, flower, or initial onto front of bag.

Making up

Fold bag in half, RS together, cast-on edge to bound-off edge, and sew both side seams with back stitch.

With a crochet hook, make a 12-in. chain and thread this through top of bag, approx. ¾ in. from top.

Fill bag with lavender or potpourri. Pull crochet chain tie to secure bag, tie in a bow or knot, and hang over hook of hanger.

PATTERN SPECIFICATIONS:

- Yarn: fingering weight mercerized cotton (or matte cotton) 1 x 2-oz. ball
- Needles: #1 (2.5 mm) and medium-size crochet hook

Gauge: 26 sts/48 rows = 4 in. in garter st.

Measurements: cover: 18 in. on top curve of coat hanger; bag: 4 x 3½ in.

Grade: 1

Note:
The hanger used here is a standard wooden hanger, 18 in. long and ¾ in. wide. Covering a hanger in this way keeps clothes from slipping off and help garments retain their shape.

Outdoors

This selection of outdoor wear will have you knitting nonstop to complete them all. The matching stocking hat, scarf, and mittens are essential, and the hats, scarves, and bags use a variety of yarns and stitches that will encourage you to try out your newly acquired skills, rewarding you with wonderful accessories for the whole family.

PATTERN SPECIFICATIONS:

Striped stocking hat
- Yarn: worsted weight yarn
  1 x 2-oz. ball MC, CC1, and
  CC2
- Needles: #7 (4.5 mm) and
  #9 (5.5 mm)

Gauge: 16–17 sts/22 rows =
4 in. over stocking stitch

Measurements: 20½ in. around

Grade: 2

Striped scarf
- Yarn: worsted weight yarn
  2 x 2-oz. balls MC and CC1;
  1 x 2-oz. ball CC2
- Needles: #7 (4.5 mm) and
  #9 (5.5 mm)

Gauge: 16–17 sts/22 rows = 4 in.

Measurements: width 9½ in.;
length 48¾ in.

Grade: 2

Key:
MC = lilac
CC1 = pink
CC2 = green

Stocking hat and scarf

Striped stocking hat

With #7 (4.5 mm) needles and MC, cast on 84 sts. Work in garter st for 1¼ in., change to #9 (5.5 mm) needles and continue in st st for 1½ in. more.
Change to CC1 and work in st st for 1½ in.
Start dec as follows:
R1: k11, *k2tog, k12, rep from * 4 times more, k2tog, k1.
R2 and alternate rows: p.
R3: k10, *k2tog, k11, rep from * 4 times more, k2tog, k1.
Rep, dec as above, until work measures 5½ in., then change to CC2. Cont dec as above until 18 sts rem. Break off yarn.

Making up

Thread end of yarn through sts with a darning needle twice and draw up tight. Sew seam using the same end and sew in any ends.

Variations

Make a hat with four or more colors by changing yarn more often.
Add a bobble (see page 103) or tassel to the top.
Work first 1¼ in. in k2, p2 rib, cable rib, or seed st.

As with other simple patterns in this book, you could substitute the worsted weight yarn with sport weight yarn and knit a hat for a child using the same pattern.

Striped scarf

With #7 (4.5 mm) needles and MC, cast on 40 sts and work 5 rows garter st.
Change to #9 (5.5 mm) needles.
R1: k4, p32, k4.
R2: k.
Rep R1–2. (This sets pattern for garter st border all around scarf.) Cont until work measures 10¼ in. Change to CC1, work for 9½ in. more. Change to CC2 and work an additional 9½ in. Change to CC1 and work 4¾ in., ending on a k row.

Start row numbering again.
R1: k4, p13, k6, p13, k4.
R2: k.
Rep R1–2.
Start split as follows:
R5: k4, p13, k3. Put rem sts on st holder and cont working with 20 sts on needle.
R6: k.

R7: k4, p13, k3.
R8: k.
Rep R7 and 8 for 4½ in., ending at inner edge.
Put these 20 sts onto a 2nd st holder and work sts from 1st st holder for 4½ in. to match, ending at outer edge.

Start row numbering again.
R1: k4, p13, k6, p13, k4.
R2: k.
Rep R1–2.
Then cont in garter stitch edging, (R1: k4, p32, k4.
R2: k.) until work measures 38½ in.

Change to MC and cont until work measures 48 in. Change to #7 (4.5 mm) needles and work 5 rows garter st, then bind off.

Making up
Sew in ends.

PATTERN SPECIFICATIONS:

- Yarn: worsted weight; this project requires less than the minimum 1-oz. ball, so you could use leftover yarn from another project.
- Needles: #7 (4.5 mm) and #9 (5.5 mm)

Gauge: 16 sts/22–24 rows = 4 in.

Measurements: length 8 (10½) in.

Grade: 3

Key:
For 3-color mittens:
MC = lilac
CC1 = pink
CC2 = green

Key:
For multicolored mittens:
MC = navy
CC1 = turquoise
CC2 = red
CC3 = orange
CC4 = yellow
CC5 = lime

Mittens

You can choose to knit the mittens plain, with wide or narrow stripes in three colors, or multicolored. The pattern below encompasses all three options, with color keys provided for three-color and multicolor versions.

With #7 (4.5 mm) needles and MC, cast on 29 (35) sts and patt as follows:
R1 (WS): p1, *k1, p1, rep from * to end.
R2: k1, *p1, k1, rep from * to end.
Rep R1–2 until work measures 2½ (3) in., ending on a WS row. End of rib here. Change to #9 (5.5 mm) needles.
R5–6: st st.
For three-color mittens, work to end of rib in MC, then, following instructions below, work 1 (2) in. in MC, change to CC1 and work 2½ (3½) in., then change to CC2 and work 2 (2¾) in. or to end.
For multicolor mittens, after row 5–6, change to CC1 and patt, changing color every 6 rows while following instructions below.

Thumb gusset

R1: k14 (17), place st marker, m1, k1, m1, place st marker, k14 (17) = 31 (37) sts.
R2 and all WS rows: p, slipping markers placed on R1.
R3: k to marker, slip marker, m1, knit to 2nd marker, m1, slip marker, k to end.
Rep R2–3 until you have 11 (13) sts between markers, then p39 (47) sts.

Palm

RS: k14 (17) sts, remove the markers, place 11 (13) sts onto st holder, k14 (17). Work on 28 (34) sts in st st until work measures 6 (9) in. from start. End on a WS row. Put a marker between the two center sts.

Top shaping

R1 (RS): ssk, k to 2 sts before marker, k2tog, sl marker, ssk, k to last 2 sts, k2tog.
R2: p.
Rep R1–2 2 (3) times until 16 (18) sts rem.

Start row numbering again.
R1: k2tog across work.
R2: p.
Break off yarn, leaving a 10–in. end for sewing up. Thread this end through a darning needle and then thread through the remaining sts twice and pull tightly.

Top of thumb

With RS facing, put sts from st holder onto #9 (5.5 mm) needles. Attach yarn and knit across sts.
R1: p4 (5), p2tog, p5 (6).

Work 2 (4) rows in st st.

R1: k2tog across work.

Cut yarn, leaving an 8-in. end. Thread this through a darning needle and then thread through remaining 5 (6) sts twice and pull tightly.

Making up

Using the ends of yarn, sew opening beneath thumb and remaining seams. Sew in all ends.

Coat cord (optional)

With a crochet hook and MC (you could use the yarn double), make a chain that will be long enough to thread through both sleeves and across the back of a coat. Alternatively, make a twisted cord (see page 101). Attach one end to each mitten at rib edge.

Variation

To make mittens smaller or larger, change yarn to sport weight, fingering weight, or bulky yarn, and change needle sizes accordingly.

PATTERN SPECIFICATIONS:

- Yarn: sport weight wool
  2 x 2-oz. balls MC; 1 x 2-oz.
  ball CC
- Needles: #6 (4 mm) and #4
  (3.25 mm)

Gauge: 24 sts/28 rows = 4 in.

Measurement: width 18 (21) in.;
height 8 (9) in.

Grade: 3

Key:
MC = blue
CC = cream

Ski hat

This hat comes in two sizes: child and adult.

With #6 (4 mm) needles and MC, cast on 110 (126) sts.
Work 4 (8) rows in st st, beg with a k row.
R1 (CC): k.
R2 (MC and CC): p, purl alternate sts in each color to end.
R3 (CC): k.
R4 (MC): p.
R5 (MC): k.
R6 and 12 (MC): p.
R7: *k2 in MC, k1 in CC, rep from * to last 2 sts, k2 in MC.
R8–10 (MC): st st.
R11 (CC): k.
R13 (CC): k.
R14–18 (MC): st st.
Change to #4 (3.25 mm) needles and cont with MC, work in st st for 21 (25)
rows.
Then work 19 rows in k1, p1 rib.
Change to #6 (4 mm) needles and cont in st st (beg with p row) for 7 (9) more
rows.
Start row numbering again.
R1 (MC and CC): k, changing yarn for each st.
R2 (MC and CC): p, changing yarn for each st.
R3–6 (CC): st st.
Then follow graph for snowflake, rep pattern twice across work between points
C and D for smaller size (55 sts x 2) and between points A and B for larger size
(73 sts x 2), for 13 rows, working snowflakes in MC.
Then work 4 rows st st in CC.
Start row numbering again.
R1 (MC and CC): p, changing yarn for each st.
R2 (MC and CC): k, changing yarn for each st.
R3–7 (11) (MC): st st.
Bind off.

Making up
Fold work in half, vertical edge to vertical edge, RS facing RS. Sew side seam and
top seam. Turn up hem, sewing cast-on edge to beg of rib, then fold this section
up over rib.

For a cord tie, using a piece of MC yarn 10 ft. long, follow instructions on page
101 and sew cord to a corner of hat. Repeat for second tie. Pull corners in and
tie with a knot or bow.

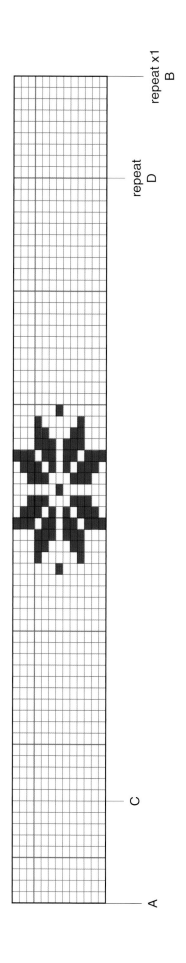

repeat x1
B

repeat
D

C

A

Making a cord tie

1 Measure a piece of thread eight times as long as the cord length required. Fold it in half, then in half again (four ends together). Hold it firmly at one end, then twist the other end very tightly in a clockwise direction. (The tighter the twist, the better the cord will be.)

2 Fold it in half again, and the cord will twist together. Tie a knot at one end.

PATTERN SPECIFICATIONS:

- Yarn: worsted weight tweed 4 x 2-oz. balls
- Needles: #7 (4.5 mm), #9 (5.5 mm), and dpn

Gauge: 16 sts/22 rows = 4 in. in st st

Measurements: diameter 20 in. (will stretch comfortably to 28-in. depth with rib turned up 9 in.)

Grade: 5

Bobble hat

Leave a 16-in. end for sewing up, then with #7 (4.5 mm) needles cast on 100 sts.
R1: *p1, k2, rep from * to last st, p1.
R2: *k1, p2, rep from * to last st, k1.
Work in this rib for 6¼ in.

Change to #9 (5.5 mm) needles.
R1: k1, p3, m1 in next st, p4, (k1, p1) 5 times, *k1, p9, (k1, p1) 5 times, rep from * 3 times, k1.
R2: *p1, k2, (p1, k1) twice, p1, k2, p1, k3, sl next 3 sts onto dpn and cable back, k3, k3 from dpn, rep from * 4 times, p1.
R3 and alternate rows: *k1, p9, (k1, p1) 5 times, rep from * 4 times more, k1.
R4 and 8: *p1, k2, (p1, k1) twice, p1, k2, p1, k9, rep from * 4 times more p1.
R6: *p1, k2, (p1, k1) twice, p1, k2, p1, sl next 3 sts onto dpn and cable front, k3, k3 from dpn, k3, rep from * 4 times more, p1.
Rep R2–9.
R18: *p1, ssk, (p1, k1) twice, p1, k2tog, p1, k3, sl next 3 sts onto dpn and cable back, k3, (k2tog, k1) from dpn, rep from * to last st, p1.
R19 and 21: *k1, p8, k1, p2, k1, p1, k1, p2, rep from * to last st, k1.
R20: *(p1, k1) 4 times, p1, k8, rep from * to last st, p1.
R22: *(p1, k1) 4 times, p1, sl next 3 sts onto dpn and cable front, k1, k2tog, k3 from dpn, k2, rep from * to last st, p1.
R23: *k1, p7, k1, p2, k1, p1, k1, p2, rep from * to last st, k1.
R24: *p1, ssk, k1, p1, k1, k2tog, p1, k7, rep from * to last st, p1.
R25: *k1, p7, (k1, p1) 3 times, rep from last st, k1.
R26: *p1, (k2, p1) twice, k2, slip next 3 sts onto dpn and cable back, k2, (k2tog, k1) from dpn, rep from * to last st, p1.
R27: *k1, p6, (k1, p1) 3 times, rep from * to last st, k1.
R28: *p1, (k2, p1) twice, sl next 2 sts onto dpn and cable front, k2tog, k2 from dpn, k2, rep from * to last st, p1.
R29: *k1, p5, (k1, p1) 3 times, rep from * to last st, k1.
R30: *p1, ssk, p1, k2tog, p1, k1, sl next 2 sts onto dpn and cable back, k2, k2tog from dpn, rep from * to last st, p1.
R31: *k1, p4, k1, p3, rep from * to last st, k1.
R32: *p1, (sl 1, k2tog, psso), p1, sl next st onto dpn and cable front, k2tog, k1 from dpn, k1, rep from * to last st, p1.
R33: *k1, p3tog, k1, p1, rep from * to last st, k1.
Slip all sts onto opposite needle and cut yarn, leaving a 20-in. end. Thread this through sts with a darning needle twice, draw up tight, and use end to sew side seam. Sew in any ends.

For a child's hat, follow the pattern using sport weight or fingering weight wool and change needle sizes accordingly.

Making a bobble

1   Cut two circles of cardboard to whatever diameter of bobble you require, and cut a circular hole in the center approximately 1¼ in. in diameter (or smaller for finer yarn). Alternatively, you can use a bobble maker, as shown here.

2   Put the two pieces of cardboard together and wrap the yarn around the cardboard, threading it through the hole in the center. The easiest way to do this is to wrap the yarn around a small piece of cardboard and pass this through the hole, unraveling the yarn as you go.

3   Cover the whole doughnut shape with yarn. The more yarn you use and the closer together you wrap the yarn, the fuller your bobble will be. With a sharp pair of scissors, cut the threads all around the circle on the outside edge between the two pieces of cardboard.

4   Ease the pieces of cardboard apart so that you can reach the center. Wrap a piece of yarn around the center and tie it in a tight and secure knot. Leave long ends on the knot and use these to attach the bobble to your main work.

5   Cut away and remove the cardboard. Fluff up the bobble, trimming the ends if necessary for a neat finish. Make a bobble in a contrasting color or use a selection of colors for a rainbow bobble.

Mohair rib scarf

With CC, cast on 44 sts and work the pattern as follows:

R1: *k1, p1, k1, p1, k1, p1, k1, p1, k4, rep from * twice more, then (k1, p1) 4 times.

R2: *p1, k1, p1, k1, p1, k1, p1, k1, p4, rep from * twice, then (p1, k1) 4 times.

Rep R1–2 twice more.

Change to MC and patt for 2 rows, then change to CC and patt for 2 rows.

Change to MC and patt for 10 rows, then change to CC and patt for 2 rows.

Change to MC and patt until work measures 55 in., then change to CC and patt for 2 rows.

Change to MC and patt for 10 rows, then change to CC and patt for 2 rows.

Change to MC and patt for 2 rows, then change to CC and patt for 6 rows.

Bind off.

Finishing

Sew in ends. Brush with a teasel to fluff up nap if necessary or leave as is.

PATTERN SPECIFICATIONS:

- Yarn: mohair 3 x 2-oz. balls MC; 1 x 2-oz. ball CC
- Needles: #8 (5 mm)

Gauge: 16 sts/24 rows = 4 in. in pattern

Measurements: 10¼ x 56¾ in. (approx., as due to the nature of rib patterns, measurements may vary over longer lengths)

Grade: 2

Key:
MC = burnt orange
CC = red

Lace scarf

With MC, cast on 51 sts with #5 (3.75 mm) needles, then begin lace pattern as follows:
R1 (RS): k1, *yfd, k3, k3tog, k3, yfd, k1, rep from * to end.
R2: k.
These 2 rows form the pattern.
Rep R1–2, 5 times more. Then cont in pattern but work following color sequence:

2 rows CC1, 2 MC, 2 CC2, 2 MC, 8 CC1, 6 CC2, 2 MC, 2 CC2, 4 MC, 2 CC2, 2 MC, 6 CC1, 4 CC2, 2 CC1, 2 MC, 2 CC2, 2 MC, 2 CC1, 12 MC, 2 CC2, 12 MC, 2 CC1, 2 MC, 2 CC2, 2 MC, 2 CC2, 2 MC, 8 CC1, 6 CC2, 2 MC, 2 CC2, 2 MC, 2 CC1.

Cont patt with MC for 10½ in., then follow color sequence:
2 rows CC1, 2 MC, 2 CC2, 2 MC, 6 CC2, 8 CC1, 2 MC, 2 CC2, 2 MC, 2 CC2, 2 MC, 2 CC1, 12 MC, 2 CC2, 12 MC, 2 CC1, 2 MC, 2 CC2, 2 MC, 2 CC1, 4 CC2, 6 CC1, 2 MC, 2 CC2, 4 MC, 2 CC2, 2 MC, 6 CC2, 8 CC1, 2 MC, 2 CC2, 2 MC, 2 CC1; then patt for 12 rows in MC and bind off.

Finishing

Weave in ends, then steam or press with a damp cloth if necessary.

PATTERN SPECIFICATIONS:

- Yarn: fingering weight wool
  1 x 2-oz. ball each of MC, CC1, and CC2
- Needles: #5 (3.75 mm)

Gauge: 28 sts/32 rows = 4 in. in lace pattern

Measurements: 7 x 45 in. approx.

Grade: 4

Key:
MC = natural
CC1 = pale green
CC2 = peat

Tips

• Always work to the end of a row before you stop knitting. If you finish in the middle of a row, you may find that a loop appears when you continue because the work has stretched. You could also lose your place in the row and this will muddle your pattern.

• When coming toward the end of a ball of yarn, try to anticipate whether it will complete a row. If not, leave the end and begin a new row with a new ball.

• Avoid tying a knot in the middle of your work, as this invariably shows from the right side and can also break and make a hole.

Textured backpack

PATTERN SPECIFICATIONS:

- Yarn: Jacob's worsted weight 2 x 2-oz. balls MC and CC1
- Needles: #7 (4.5 mm)

Gauge: 16 sts/22–23 rows = 4 in.

Measurements: width 11½ in.; length 14 in. when sewn up

Grade: 2

Key:
MC = Jacob's worsted weight
CC = ecru worsted weight

Jacob's sheep are a natural earthy brown color, so the wool is left undyed, giving an authentically rustic effect.

With MC, cast on 97 sts. Work in st st for 2½ in., then change to CC and work chevron pattern as follows:

R1 and 10: k1 *p7, k1, rep from * 11 times.
R2 and 9: p1, *k7, p1, rep from * 11 times.
R3 and 12: k2, *p5, k3, rep from * 10 times, ending with p5, k2.
R4 and 11: p2, *k5, p3, rep from * 10 times, ending with k5, p2.
R5 and 14: k3, *p3, k5, rep from * 10 times, ending with p3, k3.
R6 and 13: p3, *k3, p5, rep from * 10 times, ending with k3, p3.
R7 and 16: k4, *p1, k7, rep from * 10 times, ending with p1, k4.
R8 and 15: p4, *k1, p7, rep from * 10 times, ending with k1, p4.
Repeat R1–16 twice more.
Change back to MC and then cont in st st until work measures 12½ in.
Work 2½ in. of st st on 48 sts (putting rem 49 sts onto st holder), then bind off. Pick up rem 49 sts and work 2½ in. of st st, then bind off.

Strap
With MC, cast on 10 sts and work in k1, p1 rib for 55 in., then bind off.

Making up
To make first channel, fold over 1¼ in. from 48 st, bind off edge, WS to WS, then catch stitch it into place. Rep on 49 st and bind off edge to make second channel. Fold work in two, RS to RS, and sew bag-side seam with back stitch, ending at channel. Thread strap through both channels then through first channel again. The straps now appear at either end of work. Sew bottom seam, attaching straps into seam securely at each corner edge of bag.

Denim all-in-one bag

With #5 (3.75 mm) needles and MC, cast on 64 sts and work 2 rows garter st. Then work in st st for 1½ in., ending on a p row.

R1: k22, bind off 20 sts, k to end.

R2: p22, cast on 20 sts, p to end.

These two rows make the split handle.

Work ½ in. more in st st., then change to #6 (4 mm) needles and cont in st st for 98 rows.

Follow graph, beg at bottom right corner. Work 31 sts, then change to CC for 32nd stitch. Cont in intarsia (do not pass yarn across back of work) with MC and CC. Follow graph for 73 rows. Then cont with MC in st st for 9 rows. Change to #5 (3.75 mm) needles and work ½ in. in st st, ending on a p row.

Rep R1–2 (above) to make second handle.

Work in st st for 1½ in., ending on a p row. Work 2 rows garter st. Bind off.

Making up

Weave in ends of flower motif. Fold work in half, RS together and bound-off edge to bound-off edge. Sew side seams, then fold in bottom corners to strengthen base of bag. Sew 2½ in. across each corner to make a triangle inside the bag (see illustration). Wash bag at a warm temperature: this will shrink it in length by 20 percent. (It can be washed at a hotter temperature to firm up work.) Lining the bag with fabric will keep it from stretching and help it last longer.

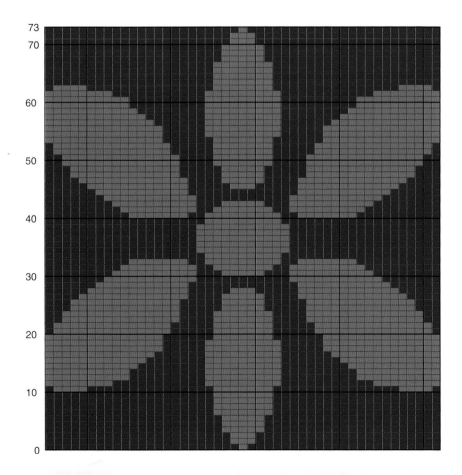

PATTERN SPECIFICATIONS:

- Yarn: sport weight denim 3 x 2-oz. balls MC; 1 x 2-oz. ball CC
- Needles: #5 (3.75 mm) and #6 (4 mm)

Gauge: 22 sts/30 rows = 4 in. in st st (when washed)

Measurements: length 15 in.; width 11 in. (when washed)

Grade: 3

Key:
MC = dark denim
CC = light denim

Note:
When washed, denim yarn shrinks by approx. 20 percent, in length only (this figure varies depending on the temperature of wash and differing washing machine cycles), and the pattern allows for this shrinkage. If you want to make the bag in plain sport weight cotton, reduce the overall length by 20 percent.

PATTERN SPECIFICATIONS:

- Yarn: sport weight tweed 10 x 2-oz. balls
- Needles: #6 (4 mm)

Gauge: 20 sts/30 rows = 4 in.

Measurements: width 70 in.; length 19 in.

Grade: 4

Shawl

Cast on 92 sts and work 8 rows in garter st.
R9: k.
R10: k6, p80, k6.
Rep R9–10.

Start patterned rib border

R1 (RS): k.
R2 and 14: k.
R3 and 13: k6, *k4, (p1, k5) twice, rep from * 4 times more, k6.
R4 and 12: k6, *(p3, k1) 3 times, p4, rep from * 4 times more, k6.
R5 and 11: k6, *k2, p1, k3, p1, k1, (p1, k3) twice, rep from * 4 times more, k6.
R6 and 10: k6, *p1, k1, (p3, k1) 3 times, p2, rep from * 4 times more, k6.
R7 and 9: k6, *p1, k3, p1, k5, p1, k3, p1, k1, rep from * 4 times more, k6.
R8: k6, *p3, k1, p7, k1, p3, k1, rep from * 4 times more, k6.
Rep R3–14 once more.
Next row: k.
Next row: k6, p80, k6.
Rep the last two rows once more.

Start embossed leaf pattern

R1, 3, 4, 16: k6, p80, k6.
R2 and 10: k.
R5: k6, *p5, k5, rep from * 7 times more, k6.
R6 and 11: k6, *k1, p5, k4, rep from * 7 times more, k6.
R7 and 12: k6, *p3, k5, p2, rep from * 7 times more, k6.
R8 and 13: k6, *k3, p5, k2, rep from * 7 times more, k6.
R9 and 14: k6, *p1, k5, p4, rep from * 7 times more, k6.
R15: k6 *k5, p5, rep from * 7 times more, k6.
Rep R1–16, 4 times.
Next row: k.
Next row: k6, p80, k6.
Rep last two rows once more.

Start Vandyke check pattern

R1 and 7: k.
R2, 8, 9, 10, 11, 17: k6, *k4, p4, rep from * 9 times, k6.
R3: k6, p1, *k4, p4, rep from * 8 times, k4, p3, k6.
R4: k8, *p4, k4, rep from * 8 times, p4, k8.
R5: k6, p3, *k4, p4, rep from * 8 times, k4, p1, k6.
R6, 13, 19, 20, 21, 22: k6, *p4, k4, rep from * 9 times, k6.
R12 and 18: k6, p80, k6.
R14: k7, *p4, k4, rep from * 8 times, p4, k9.

R15: k6, p2, *k4, p4, rep from * 8 times, k4, p2, k6.

R16: k9, *p4, k4, rep from * 8 times, p4, k7.

Rep R1–22 3 times.

R23: k.

R24: k6, p80, k6.

Rep last two rows once more.

Work embossed leaf pattern R1–16 6 times, then rep the last two rows twice.

Work Vandyke check pattern R1–22 4 times, then rep the last two rows twice.

Work embossed leaf pattern R1–16 5 times.

Next row: *k6, p80, k6.

Next row: k.

Next row: k6, p80, k6.*

Next 2 rows: k.

Repeat from * to * once.

Work patterned rib border pattern R3–14, twice, then work the last two rows twice.

Finally, k 8 rows, and bind-off.

PATTERN SPECIFICATIONS:

- Yarn: Jacob's worsted weight
  4 x 2-oz. balls MC; 1 x 2-oz.
  ball CC
- Needles: #8 (5 mm)

Gauge: 17–18 sts/30 rows = 4 in.
in garter st

Measurements: body length 23 in.
at longest point; strap length
26¼ in. (unstretched); width 2½ in.

Grade: 2

Key:
MC = Jacob's worsted weight
CC = red worsted weight

Dog coat

With MC, cast on 74 sts and work 18 rows in garter st.
R19: k2, inc in next st, k to last 3 sts, inc in next st, k2 = 76 sts.
Work in garter st, inc 1 st at each end of every 19th row (on 3rd st from edge,
fully fashioned increasing) until = 88 sts, then work 7 more rows = 140 rows.

Start row numbering again.

R1: k34, keep rem 54 sts on a st holder.
Turn, working one side at a time.
R2: k2, k2tog, k2tog, k to end = 32 sts.
R3 and alternate rows: k.
R4: k2 k2tog, k2tog, k to end = 30 sts.
R6: k2 k2tog, k2tog, k to end = 28 sts.
R8: k2 k2tog, k2tog, k to end = 26 sts.
R10: k2, k2tog, k to end = 25 sts.
R12: k2, k2tog, k to end = 24 sts.
R14: k2, k2tog, k to last 3 sts, inc in next st, k2 = 24 sts.
Cont dec on inside edge every other row until 15 sts rem.
R23: k2, k2tog, k to last 3 sts, inc. in next st, k2 = 15 sts.
R24, 26, 28: k.
R25: k2, k2tog, k to end = 14 sts.
R27: k2, k2tog, k to end = 13 sts.
Bind-off rem 13 sts.

Starting from inside edge, bind off 20 sts, k34, turn.
R1: k to last 6 sts, k2tog, k2tog, k2 = 32 sts.
R2 and alternate rows: k.
R3: k to last 6 sts, k2tog, k2tog, k2 = 30 sts.
R5: k to last 6 sts, k2tog, k2tog, k2 = 28 sts.
R7: k to last 6 sts, k2tog, k2tog, k2 = 26 sts.
R9: k to last 4 sts, k2tog, k2 = 25 sts.
R11: k to last 4 sts, k2tog, k2 = 24 sts.
R12: k2, inc in next st, k to last 4 sts, k2tog, k2 = 24 sts.
R13: k.
Cont dec on inside edge every other row until 15 sts rem.

Start row numbering again.
R1: k2, inc in next st, k to last 4 sts, k2tog, k2 = 15 sts.
Make a buttonhole as follows:
R2: k5, bind off 4 sts, k to end.
R3: k6, cast on 4 sts, k1, k2tog, k2 = 14 sts.

R4 and 6: k.
R5: k to last 4 sts, k2tog, k2 = 13sts.
Bind off rem 13 sts.

Strap

With CC, cast on 11 sts and work ⅝ in. in garter st.
R1: k4, bind off 3 sts, k to end.
R2: k4, cast on 3 sts, k to end.
Work ⅝ in. more in garter st, then rep R1 and 2.
Work in garter st until strap measures 26¼ in., then
bind off.

Making up

Attach strap by placing it lengthwise onto main body, 8½ in.
from cast-on edge of coat's body. Bound-off edge of band
should be 2½ in. in from left edge of coat. Sew band
securely at center of work only.

Sew two buttons in place at bound-off edge of strap,
matching position of buttonholes. This allows two settings
for width of dog coat.

TIP

• When knitting for children or animals, weave in any loose ends securely so that you do not leave
threads dangling inside a garment. Any long threads or loops may become caught up during wear and
cause the knitting to unravel.

Grown-ups

Following is a stunning selection of classic designs that you will want to knit and wear year after year. These timeless styles encourage the development of your knitting expertise by incorporating the techniques you have learned at the beginning of the book. There is no reason why you shouldn't adapt the patterns to suit your own individual style, changing yarn texture and colors to match your existing wardrobe.

PATTERN SPECIFICATIONS:

- Yarn: sport weight cotton
  7 x 2 oz. balls MC; 5 x 2 oz.
  balls CC1; 4 x 2-oz. balls
  CC2
- Needles: #4 (3.25 mm), #6
  (4 mm), and #7 (4.5 mm); also
  flexible needle #7 (4.5 mm)

Gauge: 21 sts/39 rows = 4 in. in
pattern

Measurements (without fringe):
length from shoulder to bottom
point 33½ in.; width at widest
point 32 in. (These measurements
are approx., as the nature of a
poncho style using a chevron-style
pattern means that the weight of
the yarn may affect the finished
length and width.)

Grade: 5

Key:
MC = grape
CC1 = blue
CC2 = burnt orange

Poncho

Notes

With 299 sts on your needles, you need to begin with circular needles, then change to ordinary needles when appropriate.

As you are working three color stripes, do not break yarn off after every 2nd row, but carry it up the side of your work evenly with the length of your work. This keeps your work neat and you will have fewer ends to sew in.

The back and front are the same.

With the circular needles and CC1, cast on 299 sts and patt as follows:
R1 (RS): k3, *wyib, sl 1, k3, rep from * to end.
R2: k3, *yfd, sl 1, yb, k3, rep from * to end.
R3 (CC2): k1, *wyib, sl 1, k3, rep from * to last 2 sts, yb, sl 1, k1.
R4 (CC2): k1, *yfd, sl 1, yb, k3, rep from * to last 2 sts, yfd, sl 1, yb, k1.
R5 (MC): work as R1.
R6 (MC): patt 148 sts, k3tog (or sl 1, k2tog, psso if you find it easier), patt 148.
R7 (CC1): patt 146, k1, k3tog, k1, patt 146.
R8 (CC1): patt 146, k3tog, patt 146.
R9 (CC2): patt 144, k1, k3tog, k1, patt 144.
R10 (CC2): patt 144, k3tog, patt 144.
R11 (MC): patt 142, k1, k3tog, k1, patt 142.
R12 (MC): patt 142, k3tog, patt 142.
R13 (CC1): patt 140, k1, k3tog, k1, patt 140.
R14 (CC1): patt 140, k3tog, patt 140.
R15 (CC2): patt 138, k1, k3tog, k1, patt 138.
R16 (CC2): patt 138, k3tog, patt 138.
R17 (MC): patt 136, k1, k3tog, k1, patt 136.
R18 (MC): patt 275.
R19 (CC1): patt 275.
R20 (CC1): patt 275.
R21 (CC2): patt 275.
Cont in this way, dec 2 sts at center of first 12 rows of pattern, then working 4 rows straight, changing colors every 2 rows as set.
Work until 83 sts rem, then continue with 4 straight rows ending on R21 of pattern.
Dec 2 sts at center of next 3 rows = 77 sts.
You should be using CC1 at this point and have RS facing.

Neck band

Change to #4 (3.25 mm) needles, and with CC1 work 8 rows in garter st, still dec 2 sts at center of each row = 61 sts. Bind off.

Making up

Sew side seams with mattress st.

Fringe

With MC and #6 (4 mm) needles, cast on 11 sts.

R1: k2, yon, k2tog, k1, yon, k2tog, k4.

R2: p3, k2, (yon, k2tog, k1) twice.

Rep these 2 rows until the fringe measures all around the poncho and allowing extra to be eased around the corners. End with a R2.

Next row: sl 1 st, bind off next 7 sts, draw yarn through, then break off. Drop rem 3 sts off needle, then unravel back to the beg. This makes the fringe part of the edging.

Variation

Use 5 colors instead of 3, working the pattern as set but changing color every 2 rows (see above right).

Tips

• Leave up to a 16-inch tail when your yarn ends on a side that is going to become a seam. This can later be used for sewing up your work.

• Be aware that constant stretching can break the edges of your work.

Ribbed vest

This comes in both women's and men's sizes; men's sizes are in parentheses.

Back

With #3 (3.25 mm) needles, cast on 91 (112) sts and work in k1, p1 rib for 1 in. Change to #5 (3.75 mm) needles and work as follows:

R1: *k2, p1, k1, p1, k2, rep from * to end.
R2: *p3, k1, p3, rep from * to end.
These 2 rows form the pattern.
R3: k1, m1 in next st, p1, k1, p1, k2, *k2, p1, k1, p1, k2, rep from *
10 (13) times more, k2, p1, k1, p1, m1 in next st, k1 = 93 (114) sts.
Continue following R1 and 2 for pattern, increasing every 8th row
(as described in R3) until 109 (130) sts.
Cont until work measures 9½ (11) in., and end on a WS row.

Start armhole shaping

Cont in pattern, bind off 4 sts at beg of following 8 rows = 77 (98) sts.
Next row: dec 1 st at either end of this row and then every alternate row
8 times = 59 (80) sts.
Cont in pattern until work measures 17¼ (20) in.

Start shoulder shaping

Cont in pattern, bind off 4 (5) sts at beg of next 2 rows,
then bind off 5 (6) sts at beg of next 4 rows.
For women's size, bind off 31 sts for back neck.
For men's size, bind off only 6 sts at each end and bind off
remaining 34 sts for back neck.

Pocket linings (make 2)

With #3 (3.25 mm) needles, cast on 20 (26) sts and work in st st for 3 in.,
finishing with a p row. Keep sts on a st holder.

Right front

With #3 (3.25 mm) needles, cast on 43 (54) sts and work in k1, p1 rib
for 1 in. Change to #5 (3.75 mm) needles and work 2 rows in pattern.
Next row: inc 1 st on outside edge only.
Cont in pattern and inc every 8th row until work measures 4⅛ in.,
ending on WS.
Next row: patt 20 sts, slip next 20 (26) sts onto stitch holder. Cont in pattern
across sts from pocket lining and then cont across rem sts.
Cont in pattern and with increases until = 52 (63) sts.
Cont in pattern until work measures 9½ (11) in., ending on RS.

PATTERN SPECIFICATIONS:

- Yarn: sport weight wool 5 (8) x 2-oz. balls
- Needles: #3 (3.25 mm) and #5 (3.75 mm)

Gauge: 21 sts/30 rows = 4 in. in pattern

Measurements: length 17¾ (20¾) in.; chest 41¾ (50½) in. (when worn); due to the rib nature of this stitch pattern, the garment pulls in to make a fitted style.

Grade: 4

Start armhole shaping

Bind off 4 sts, on armhole edge only, on next and following 3 alternate rows = 36 (47) sts.

Next row: start V-neck shaping by dec 1 st on this row and every 4th row 13 (16) times, while cont dec on armhole edge every alternate row 8 times = 14 (22) sts.

Cont until work measures 17¼ (20¼) in., ending on outside edge.

Start shoulder shaping

R1: bind off 4 (5) sts, then patt to end.

R2: patt to last 5 (6) sts, then cast these off.

R3: patt 5 (12) sts.

R4: bind off 5 (6) sts (men's size: patt 6 sts).

R5: (men's size only) bind off 6 sts.

Left front

Work as for right front, reversing pocket placement and all shapings.

Pocket edges

With #3 (3.25 mm) needles and MC, pick up 20 (26) sts from pocket lining on st holder.

Work in k1, p1 rib for ¾ in. Bind off. Repeat for other lining.

Front bands

With #3 (3.25 mm) needles, cast on 11 sts and work in k1, p1 rib for 2 (2¾) in.

Buttonhole row: rib 4 sts, bind off 3 sts, rib to end.

Next row: rib 4 sts, cast on 3 sts, rib to end.

Cont in rib, making 4 more buttonholes at 2 (2½) in. intervals.

Then cont in k1, p1 rib until band stretches around neck and fronts when slightly stretched. Bind off.

Making up

Sew shoulder seams with neat back stitch.

With #3 (3.25 mm) needle, pick up all sts from around armhole. Work in k1, p1, rib for 2 cm, cast off.

Note: try not to cast off too tightly around armhole.

Sew front bands in place. Sew buttons on.

Note: buttonhole band can be placed on right or left side as required.

Tips

• After spending so much time knitting a garment, you'll want to always take the necessary time to prepare it properly for sewing up (see page 73) and use the correct sewing stitches and yarn to do this.

• To make neat edges for seams, you can knit the first and last stitch on every row, even when the remaining stitches are to be purled. If you use this method, which is called a "seam stitch," you need to add two extra stitches to your work.

Pockets

There are two types of pockets you could add to your knitted work: concealed pockets and patch pockets.

Concealed pocket

1 Make a pocket lining by knitting a rectangle in stockinette stitch to the width and length required, keeping the stitches on a stitch holder. Then work the garment until you reach the row that corresponds with the top of the pocket. Work the pattern to where the edge of the pocket will begin, then slip the same number of stitches as there are on the pocket top onto a separate stitch holder. Continue in pattern across the stitches from the pocket lining and then continue across the remaining stitches of the main work to the end of the row. When the pocket bag is finished, attach it to the front of your work around three sides, following the lines of the knitting to assure a straight pocket. Alternatively, you can attach the cast-on edge to your work when you reach the row where the base of the pocket will start, by working together the stitches from the main body with the cast-on edge of the pocket bag.

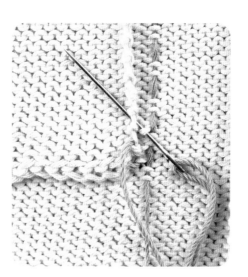

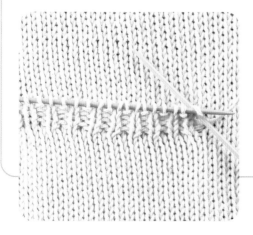

2 When the work is complete, pick up the stitches from the stitch holder and work in rib or whatever pattern is required for finishing the pocket top. Sew the pocket bag to the inside of the garment along the two sides and bottom, always trying to follow a vertical line of stitches on the side seams to ensure a straight pocket.

Patch pocket

Make a pocket by knitting a square in the stitch required for your pattern (usually stockinette stitch) and to the correct size, usually finishing with a rib. Pin the pocket into place, lining it up with the rows of knitting so that it is even on all sides. Sew with a darning needle, using the same color yarn, as shown.

PATTERN SPECIFICATIONS:

- Yarn: Worsted weight 14 x 2 oz. balls.
- Needles #9 (5.5 mm) #7 (4.5 mm)

Gauge: 16 sts/22–24 rows = 4 in.

Measurements: width 20 in. (22 in.); length 22 in. (24 in.).

Grade: 2

Notes
For cast-on edge use 2 ends of yarn, This makes a firmer edge and knitting into the back of each st on R1 gives a finished edge to work. Reverse st st is exactly that—the wrong side of stocking stitch.

For a variation, leave a side split open on the side seams when making up. Alternatively, cast on with a contrasting color to give a color-tipped effect.

Her sweater

Back

With # 7 (4.5 mm) needles and yarn used double, cast on 82 (94) sts.
R1: with single strand, k into back of each stitch.
R2: K. R3: p (RS). Change to 5.5mm needles.
R4: k, R5: p. Repeat R4 and 5 until work measures 36 (42) cm. End on a p row.
Shape armhole: cast off 5 sts at the beginning of following 2 rows.
R3: k2 k2tog to last 4sts, k2tog k2 = 70 (82) sts.
R4: p. Rep last 2 rows until 64 (76) sts.
R5: k. R6: p.
R7: k2, k2tog, k to last 4sts, k2tog,k2. Rep last 4 rows until 60 (70) sts.
Continue in reverse st st until work measures 59 (68) cm, ending on a p row.
Next row: bind off 10 (12) sts, keep 40 (42) sts on st holder, and then bind off remaining 10 (12) sts.

Front

Work as back until work measures 19$\frac{3}{4}$ in./23$\frac{1}{4}$ in. end on a p row.
R1: k16 (20) sts, keep 28 (30) sts on stitch holder, place marker, keep remaining 16 (20) sts on a stitch holder.
Working one side at a time, and starting on neck edge, R1: p.
R2: k to last 4 sts, k2tog, k2.
Rep last 2 rows 5 (6) times more = 10 (13) sts.
Work 8 rows more, then bind off 10 (13) sts.
Repeat on opposite side, picking up 16 (20) sts from st holder and leaving center 28 (30) sts on holder.

Sleeve

With #7 (4.5 mm) needles and yarn used double cast on 40 sts.
R1: using a single strand k into back of each stitch. R2:K. R3: p (RS).
Change to #9 (5.5 mm) needles
R4: k. R5: p.
R6: k2, m1 in next st k to last 3sts, m1 in next st, k2.
R7: p. R8: k.
R9: p. Rep last 6 rows until 74 (82) sts. Then cont until work measures 19 in. (19$\frac{3}{4}$ in.), ending on a p row. Bind off 6sts at the beg of next two rows = 62 (70) sts.
R1: k2, k2tog, k54 (62), k2tog, k2 = 60 (68) sts.
R2: p2, p2tog, p52 (60), p2tog, p2 = 58 (66) sts.
R3: k2, k2tog, k50 (58), k2tog, k2 = 56 (64) sts.
R4: p. R5: k2, k2tog, k48 (56) k2tog, k2 = 54 (62) sts.
Rep last 2 rows 12 times more, p one row = 30 (38) sts. Bind off.

Collar

With RS facing, sew 1 shoulder seam. Using #9 (5.5 mm) needles and with st st side (WS) facing, pick up sts around neck, beginning with 40 (42) sts from back neck, 20 (22) sts from down front neck, 28 (30) sts from stitch holder across center front and then 20 (22) sts up front side = 108 (116) sts. Work in rev st st until work measures 26 cm end on a p row. Double up yarn and cast off in knit.

Making up

Sew 2nd shoulder seam and sew seam of collar. Sew in sleeve head, match cast off edge with vertical edge, and ease in where necessary. Match dec edge to dec edge and sew side seams and sleeve side seams.

His sweater

Back

Cast on 74 sts and work in garter st for 2 in., then cont in st st for 26 in., ending on a p row. Bind off 23 sts, put center 28 sts on st holder, then bind off rem 23 sts.

Front

Work as back until work measures 16 rows shorter than back, ending on a p row. Then start dec for front neck as follows:
R1: k28, put 18 sts on st holder, add st marker, then add rem 28 sts to st holder.
R2 and 4: p.
R3: k to last 4 sts, k2tog, k2.
Rep R3–4 4 times = 23 sts. Work 4 more rows in st st, then bind off.
Rejoin yarn at marker and leave center 18 sts on st holder. K2, sl 1, k1, psso, work to end. Next row: p.
Rep last 2 rows until 23 sts rem, then work 4 rows in st st and bind-off.

Sleeves

Cast on 36 sts and work in garter st for 1¼ in. Then work in st st, beg with a k row, inc 1 st at each end of this and every 6th row until 66 sts rem. Cont until work measures 20½ in., then bind off.

Neckband

Sew left shoulder seam. With RS facing, pick up sts around neck beg with 28 sts from back neck, then 15 sts down front neck edge, 18 sts from center front, 15 sts from opposite front = 76 sts.
Work in k2, p2 rib for 1¼ in., ending with RS facing. Then work 5 rows st st and bind off. The st st section of the neck band will roll forward.

Making up

Sew 2nd shoulder seam and neckband seam, reversing st st seam to roll forward. Sew in sleeves to 10 in. below shoulder seam. Sew side seams of body and sleeve.

PATTERN SPECIFICATIONS:

- Yarn: Jacob's worsted weight (used double) 23 x 2-oz. balls
- Needles: #10.5 (6.5 mm)

Gauge: 13 sts/18 rows = 4 in.

Measurement: width 21¼ in.; length 28 in.

Grade: 2

PATTERN SPECIFICATIONS:

- Yarn: 8 oz. sport weight angora
- Needles: #3 (3.25 mm) and #6 (4 mm)

Gauge: 21 sts/29 rows = 4 in. in st st

Measurements: length 16½ in.; chest 36 in.; tie 10 ft., to go around the waist 3 times.

Grade: 5

Wrap cardigan

Notes

As this is a crossover garment, it will comfortably fit a larger chest size.
All increases and decreases are worked on the RS using the fully fashioned method (see pages 40–41): sl 1, k2tog, psso, looks very like k3tog in reverse.
If the decreasing is near the beginning of the row, it is k2tog; if it is at the end of a row, it is ssk.

Ties band

With #3 (3.25 mm) needles, cast on 10 sts and work in k1, p1 rib for 10 ft. (Try not to have joins in this length, but if this is unavoidable, join on the edge that joins to the main piece of work.) After 10 ft., put the sts on a st holder and leave a long end in case you need to make the tie longer.

Back

With #3 (3.25 mm) needles, cast on 83 sts and work in k1, p1 rib for 20 rows (RS rows end with a k1 and WS rows beg with a p1).
Change to #6 (4 mm) needles and work in st st as follows:
R21 (RS): k2, inc in next st, k to last 3 sts, inc in next st, k2.
R22: p.
Then cont in st st, inc every 8th row from previous inc, to R33.
Work 9 more rows in st st = 93 sts.
R43: bind off 2 sts (for underarm), k to end.
R44: bind off 2 sts purlwise, p to end.
R45, 49, 53, 57, 61, 65: k2, k2tog, k to last 4 sts, ssk, k2.
R46 and 48: p.
R47: k.
R66: p.
Then dec at each end of R67 and every other k row until 39 sts rem; p next row, then bind off.

Sleeves

With #3 (3.25 mm) needles, cast on 51 sts and work in k1, p1 rib for 26 rows.
With RS facing, change to #6 (4 mm) needles and work in st st.
Inc 1 st at each end of 1st row and every 12th row until you have 71 sts.
Cont in st st until sleeve measures 20 in., ending with a p row.
Bind off 2 sts at beg of next 2 rows for underarm, then dec at each end of next row and every following k row until 7 sts rem. Bind off. Rep for 2nd sleeve.

Left front

With #3 (3.25 mm) needles, cast on 71 sts.

R1, 2, 3, 4, 6, 7, 8, 10, 11, 12, 14, 15, 16, 18, 19, 20: k1, p1.

R5, 9, 13, 17: k1, p1 to last 5 sts, sl 1, k2tog, psso, p1, k1.

With RS facing, change to #6 (4 mm) needles and then cont in st st.

Start row numbering again.

R1: k2, inc in next st, k to last 5 sts, sl 1, k2tog, psso, k2.

R2 and alternate rows: p.

R3, 5, 7, 11, 13, 15: k to last 4 sts, ssk, k2.

R9 and 17: k2, inc in next st, k to last 4 sts, ssk, k2.

Cont, dec at end of every k row (neck edge) until R41, and inc at beg of R25 and 33.

R43: bind off 2 sts, k to last 4 sts, ssk, k2.

R45 and 49: k2, k2tog, k to last 4 sts, ssk, k2.

R47: k to last 4 sts, ssk, k2.

For next 16 rows, cont dec at end of every k row and beg (armhole edge) of every 4th row = 26 sts.

On the following 16 rows, change so that you dec at beg (armhole edge) of every k row and at end (neck edge) of every 4th row = 14 sts.

Cont, dec at only beg of every k row (so not at neck edge) until 3 sts rem, then p3tog. Cut off yarn, leaving a 4-in. end, and thread through last st to finish.

Right front

With #3 (3.25 mm) needles, cast on 71 sts.

R1, 2, 3, 4, 6, 7, 8, 10, 11, 12, 14, 15, 16, 18, 19, 20: k1, p1.

R5, 9, 13, 17: k1, p1, k3tog, k1, p1 to end.

With RS facing, change to #6 (4 mm) needles and then work in st st as follows:

Start row numbering again.

R1: k2, k3tog, k to last 3 sts, inc in next st, k2.

R2 and alternate rows: p.

R3, 5, 7, 11, 13, 15: k2, k2tog, k to end.

R9 and 17: k2, k2tog, k to last 3 sts, inc in next st, k2.

Cont dec at beg (neck edge) of every k row until R43, and inc at end of R25 and 33.

R44 (WS): bind off 2 sts purlwise (for underarm), p to end.

R45 and 49: k2, k2tog, k to last 4 sts, ssk, k2.

R47: k2, k2tog, k to end.

For next 16 rows, cont dec at beg (neck edge) of every k row and at end (armhole edge) of every 4th row = 26 sts.

Then, on the following 16 rows, change so that you dec at

the beg (neck edge) of every 4th row and at the end (armhole edge) of every k row = 14 sts.

Cont, dec only at end of every k row (so not at neck edge) until 3 sts rem, then p3tog. Cut off yarn, leaving a 4-in. end, and thread through last st to finish.

Making up

Join sleeves to back and fronts from underarm to neck. Use mattress stitch, working from RS, matching row for row.

Join sleeve side seams and left side seam from cast-on edge to underarm in same way.

Join right side seam of body for ¾ in. from cast-on edge and finish off securely, then leave an opening of about 1¼ in. (for tie to pull through). Cont sewing side seam, making sure there are no gaps at underarm point.

Leaving approx. 30–32 in. from beg of tie band, start joining to neck edge of one of fronts. Use angora double and relaxed mattress stitch, as this join needs flexibility. Attach around front, across back neck, and down second front, making sure remaining tie end is long enough, then cast it off. Sew in all loose ends.

Cable cardigan

Back

With #5 (3.75 mm) needles, cast on 90 sts and work 6 rows in k1, p1 rib (work should measure ¾ in.). Change to #6 (4 mm) needles and work 6 rows st st, ending on a p row.

R13: k2, k2tog, k to last 4 sts, k2tog, k2 = 88 sts.

R14: p.

Rep R13–14 6 times = 76 sts.

The cable panel

Start row numbering again.

R1, 5, 7, 11, 13, 17: k1, p1, *k1, p1, k4, p1, k1, p1, rep from * 7 times more, k1, p1.

R2, 4, 6, 8, 10, 12, 14, 16, 18: k1, p1, *k1, p1, k1, p4, k1, p1, rep from * 7 times more, k1, p1.

R3, 9, 15: k1, p1, *k1, p1, sl next 2 sts onto dpn and hold at back, k2, then k2 from dpn, p1, k1, p1, rep from * 7 times more, k1, p1.

R19: k.

R20: p.

R21: k2, m1 in next st, k to last 3 sts, m1 in next st, k2 (fully fashioned increasing) = 78 sts.

R22 and 24: p.

R23: k.

R25: k2, m1 in next st, k to last 3 sts, m1 in next st, k2 = 80 sts.

Rep R22–5 = 82 sts.

R30, 32, 34: p.

R31 and 33: k.

R35: k2, m1 in next st, k to last 3 sts, m1 in next st, k2 = 84 sts.

Rep R30–5 6 times more = 96 sts.

R72 and 74: p.

R73: k.

R75: bind off 4 sts at the beg of the next 2 rows = 88 sts.

R77: k2, k2tog, k to last 4 sts, k2tog, k2 = 86 sts.

R78: p.

Rep R77–8 3 times = 80 sts.

R85: k2, k2tog, k to last 4 sts, k2tog, k2.

R86, 88, 90: p.

R87, 89: k.

Rep R85–90 8 times = 62 sts.

Start back neck shaping

R1: k21, bind off 20 sts, put rem 21 sts on st holder.

R2 (starting on neck edge): p to end.

R3: k17, k2tog, k2 = 20 sts.

R4, 6, 8: p.

R5: k17, k2tog, k2 = 19 sts.

R7: k17, k2tog, k2 = 18 sts.

Bind off shoulder sts.

Pick up 21 sts from st holder and dec on neck edge to match opposite side.

1st front

With #5 (3.75 mm) needles, cast on 42 sts.

R1: p1, k1, p1, k4, p1, then k1, p1 to end.

R2: k1, p1 to last 8 sts, k1, p4, k1, p1, k1.

Repeat these two rows once more.

R5: p1, k1, p1, sl next 2 sts onto dpn and cable back, k2, then k2 from dpn, p1, then k1, p1 to end.

(Work should now measure ¾ in.)

Change to #6 (4 mm) needles.

R7 and 9: k2, p1, k4, p1, k to end.

R8 and 10: p to last 8 sts, k1, p4, k1, p2.

R11: k2, p1, sl next 2 sts onto dpn and hold at back, k2, then k2 from dpn, p1, k to end.

R12: p to last 8 sts, k1, p4, k1, p2.

R13: k2, p1, k4, p1, k to last 4 sts, k2tog, k2 = 41 sts.

Cont as set, dec on outside edge every 2nd row and cabling every 6th row until 35 sts rem.

Work 1 more row.

Work as follows for the cable panel:

R1, 5, 7, 11, 13, 17: p1, *k1, p1, k4, p1, k1, p1, rep from * twice, then k1, p1 to end.

R2, 4, 6, 8, 10, 12, 14, 16, 18: p1, k1, p1, k1, p1, k1, p1, *k1, p1, k1, p4, k1, p1, rep from * twice, k1.

R3, 9, 15: p1, *k1, p1, sl next 2 sts onto dpn and cable back, k2, then k2 from dpn, p1, k1, p1, rep from * twice, then k1, p1 to end.

Then cont in st st.

R19: k2, p1, k4, p1, k to end.

R20: p to last 8 sts, k1, p4, k1, p2.

Cont cabling every 6 rows.

R21: k2, p1, k4, p1, k to last 3 sts, m1 in next st, k2 (fully fashioned increasing) = 36 sts.

R22 and 24: p to last 8 sts, k1, p4, k1, p2.

R23: k2, p1, k4, p1, k to end.

R25: k2, p1, k4, p1, k to last 3 sts, m1 in next st, k2 = 37 sts.

Rep R22–5 = 38 sts.

R30, 32, 34: p to last 8 sts, k1, p4, k1, p2.

R31 and 33: k2, p1, k4, p1, k to end.

R35: k2, p1, k4, p1, k to last 3 sts, m1 in next st, k2 = 39 sts.

Rep R30–5 6 times more (36 rows) = 45 sts.

R86 and 88: p to last 8 sts, k1, p4, k1, p2.

R87 and 89: k2, p1, k4, p1, k to end.

Then bind-off 4 sts at the beginning of following row, work to end of row, continue working cable as set = 40 sts.

*** Next row: work to last 4 sts, k2tog, k2 = 39 sts

Next row: p and work cable as set.**

Repeat from *** to ** twice more = 37 sts.

Next row: work to last 4sts, k2tog, k2,

Work next 5 rows in st st, continuing cable as set = 36 sts.

Repeat last 6 rows 4 times more. 24 rows = 32 sts.

Start front neck shaping.

R1 (beg on neck edge): bind off 2 sts, k to last 4 sts, k2tog, k2 = 29 sts.

R2, 4, 6: p.

R3 and 5: k2, k2tog, k to end.

R7: k2, k2tog, k to last 4 sts, k2tog, k2 = 25 sts.

R8–10: work 3 rows st st.

R11: k2, k2tog, k to end = 24 sts.

R12 and 14: p.

R13: k to last 4 sts, k2tog, k2 = 23 sts.

R15: k2, k2tog, k to end = 22 sts.

R16–18: 3 rows st st.

R19: k2, k2tog, k to last 4 sts, k2tog, k2 = 20 sts.

Rep R16–18.

R23: k2, k2tog, k to end = 19 sts.

Rep R16–18.

R27: k2, k2tog, k to end = 18 sts.

Rep R16–18 twice.

R31: bind off 18 sts.

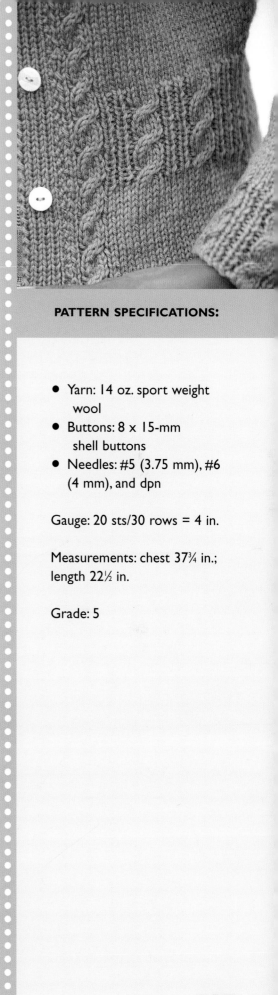

PATTERN SPECIFICATIONS:

- Yarn: 14 oz. sport weight wool
- Buttons: 8 x 15-mm shell buttons
- Needles: #5 (3.75 mm), #6 (4 mm), and dpn

Gauge: 20 sts/30 rows = 4 in.

Measurements: chest 37¾ in.; length 22½ in.

Grade: 5

2nd front

Work as 1st front but reverse all shaping and cable it so that it is the mirror image of the first front.

Sleeves

With #5 (3.75 mm) needles, cast on 55 sts.

R1 and 3: p1, k1, p1, *k4, p1, k1, p1, k1, p1, rep from * 4 times more, then k4, p1, k1, p1.

R2, 4, 6: k1, p1, k1, p4, *k1, p1, k1, p1, k1, p4, rep from * 4 times more, then k1, p1, k1.

R5: p1, k1, p1, *sl next 2 sts onto dpn and cable back, k2, then k2 from dpn, p1, k1, p1, k1, p1, rep from * 4 times, then sl next 2 sts onto dpn and cable back, k2, then k2 from dpn, p1, k1, p1.

Rep R1–6 twice, then R1–2 once.

Change to #6 (4 mm) needles.

R21: k, inc 1 st at beg = 56 sts.

R22: p.

R23: k2, m1 in next st, k to last 3 sts, m1 in next st, k2 = 58 sts.

R24 and 26: p.

R25 and 27: k.

Rep R22–7 16 times = 90 sts.

Cont in st st until work measures 17¼ in., ending on a p row.

Start sleeve head shaping.

R1: bind off 4 sts, then k to end.

R2: cast on 4 sts, then p to end = 82 sts.

R3: k2, k2tog, k74, k2tog, k2 = 80 sts.

R4: p2, p2tog, p72, p2tog, p2 = 78 sts.

R5: k2, k2tog, k70, k2tog, k2 = 76 sts.

R6: p.

Rep R5–6 13 times, then bind off rem 50 sts.

Neck band

Sew shoulder seams with mattress st or neat back st. Try to keep seams as flat as possible. With #5 (3.75 mm) needles, pick up sts around neck, beg at front edge. Pick up the 2 bound off sts, then 29 sts up neck edge, then 3 sts from edge of back neck, then 20 sts across back neck, then 3 sts from back neck edge, then rem 29 sts down second front neck, and the 2 rem bound off sts = 88 sts.

Work in k1, p1 rib for 1 in., then bind off in rib.

Front bands

Make the button band.

With #5 (3.75 mm) needles, cast on 10 sts and work in k1, p1 rib until band measures length of front when slightly stretched. Bind off in rib.

Make the buttonhole band

Cast on as for button band and work 4 rows in k1, p1 rib.

R5: k1, p1, k1, bind off 3 sts, rib to end.

R6: k1, p1, k1, p1, cast on 3 sts, rib to end. This makes a buttonhole.

Cont in rib for 3 in., then make a buttonhole following R5–6, then cont making 5 more buttonholes every 8th row, until band measures length of front, from hem to start of neck band, when slightly stretched. Rib ½ in. more, then make a buttonhole; work ⅝ in. and bind off in rib.

Making up

Sew in sleeves, matching bound-off sts from sleeve to those on front and back pieces.

Sew side seams.

Pin front bands in place and attach.

Sew on 8 x ⅝-in. shell buttons.

Tip
• To keep looping (baggy stitches) from occurring at the end of your work, slip the first stitch of each row onto the right needle, then continue in the pattern.

PATTERN SPECIFICATIONS:

- Yarn: sport weight mercerized cotton 10 x 2-oz. balls
- Needles: #5 (3.75 mm)

Gauge: 22–24 sts/28 rows = 4 in.

Measurements: width 18⅛ in; length 19¼ (24) in.

Grade: 3

Back-opening cardigan

This sweater comes in two lengths.

Front

Cast on 102 sts and work 1 in. in garter st. Then work in st st for 64 (96) rows until work measures 10 (14½) in. from cast-on edge, ending on a p row.

Start armhole shaping.
Continuing in st st, bind off 5 sts at beg of next 2 rows (92 sts), then dec (using fully fashioned method, see page 41) 1 st at each end on next and following 5 alternate rows = 80 sts. Cont until work measures 15¼ (20) in., ending on a p row.

Start front neck shaping.
R1: k27, put rem 53 sts on st holder.
R2 and 4: p.
R3: k to last 4 sts, ssk, k2.
Rep R3 and 4, 4 times more.
R5: k to last 4 sts, ssk, k2.
R6 and 8: p.
R7: k.
Rep R5–8 twice more = 19 sts.
Work 6 more rows, then cast off 19 sts.

Start row numbering again.
R1: starting at neck edge, keep 26 sts at center on st holder and k to end 27 sts on needle.
R2 and 4: p.
R3: k2, k2tog, k to end.
Rep R3 and 4 4 times more.
R5: k2, k2tog, k to end.
R6 and 8: p.
R7: k.
Rep R5–8 twice more = 19 sts.
Work 6 more rows, then bind off 19 sts.

1st back

Cast on 72 sts and work 1 in. in garter st.
R1 (RS): k.
R2: k6, p66.
Rep R1–2 31 times to make 64 rows of st st (plus an extra 32 rows for longer length), ending on a WS row.

Start armhole shaping.

R1: bind off 5 sts, k to end = 67 sts.

R2: k6, p61.

Then dec (using fully fashioned method) 1 st at armhole edge on 6 alternate rows = 61 sts.

Cont until work measures same as front—19¼ (24 in.)—ending on a p row. Then bind off 19 sts, keeping 42 sts on a st holder.

2nd back

Cast on 61 sts and work 1 in. in garter st.

R1 (RS): k.

R2: p55, k6.

Rep R1–2 7 times to make 16 rows of st st with garter st border.

R17: k8, m1 in next st, k to end = 62 sts.

R18: p56, k6.

Cont inc on inside edge on rows 27 (30), 37 (43), 47 (56), 57 (69), but note that armhole shaping—see below—starts on R66 (98), 67 (82), 77 (95), 87 (108), 97 (121), 107 (134), and 117 (147).

Start armhole shaping.

R66 (98): bind off 5 sts, p to last 6 sts, k6.

Then dec (using fully fashioned method) 1 st at armhole edge on next plus following 5 alternate rows. (Note that these 12 rows will encompass R67 and 77 on the shorter length and R108 on the longer length, where increases will be made [see above].) You should now have 57 (58) sts.

Cont, inc every 10th (13th) row until you have 61 sts and work measures 19¼ (24) in., ending on a WS row.

Put 42 sts on st holder and bind off rem 19 sts.

Sleeves

Cast on 54 sts and work 1 in. in garter st.

R1: k2, m1 in next st, k to last 3 sts, m1 in next st, k2.

Work next 5 rows in st st.

Rep R1–6 until you have 96 sts. Cont until sleeve measures 19¼ in, ending on a p row.

Bind off 5 sts at beg of next 2 rows (86 sts) then dec (using fully fashioned method) 1 st at each end on next and following 5 alternate rows (74 sts). Bind off and sew shoulder seams.

Neck band

With RS facing, pick up 42 sts from 2nd back st holder, then 28 sts from down front neck, 26 sts from front st holder, 28 sts from up front neck, and rem 42 sts from st holder (166 sts).

Work ½ in. in garter st.

R1 (RS): k4, bind off 2 sts, k34 (inc. st used to bind off), bind off 2 sts, k to end.

R2: k124, cast on 2 sts, k34, cast on 2 sts, k4.

Work ½ in. more in garter st, then bind off.

Making up

Sew in sleeves, and sew side seams.

Sew on 2¾-in. shell buttons at either end of back neck at shoulder point.

Little people

A heavenly range of designs for infants on up. The temptation to knit glorious gifts like the cot blanket make this section hard to resist, while the booties, bonnet, and mittens are a must for a newborn. The simplicity of the all-sizes sweater and the appeal of the pinafore make these classics that will be passed down from one child to another.

PATTERN SPECIFICATIONS:

- Yarn: fingering weight mercerized cotton 1 x 1-oz. ball
- Needles: #1 (2.25 mm)

Gauge: 36 sts/64 rows = 4 in. in garter st

Measurements: toe to heel 4⅛ in.

Grade: 2

Booties

Cast on 22 sts and work in garter st as follows:

R1: k, inc 1 st at each end.

R2: k.

Rep R1–2 7 times = 38 sts.

R17: k, dec 1 st at each end.

R18: k.

Rep R17–18 7 times = 22 sts.

R33: cast on 8 more sts (for heel) = 30 sts.

R34 and alternate rows to R50: keeping heel edge straight, inc 1 st at other end (toe) = 38 sts.

R35 and alternate rows to R49: k.

R51: bind off 20 sts at heel edge, then k to end.

Work 19 rows (2 in.) on rem 18 sts, casting on 20 sts at end of last row = 38 sts.

Cont knitting, keeping heel edge straight, and dec 1 st at toe edge on alternate rows until 30 sts rem. Bind off.

Making up

Sew together the two straight edges of heel and sew edges of sole together, easing in fullness at toe.

Strap

With RS facing, k18 sts at heel (9 sts at each side of joining), then cast on 14 sts, k back, then cast on 14 sts at other end.

R2, 3, 6, 7, 8: k.

R4: k2, bind off 3 sts, k to end.

R5: k to end, casting on 3 sts over those cast off on R4.

Work 2nd bootie in same way, working buttonhole on strap at opposite end of needle.

Sew on buttons to correspond with buttonholes.

Variations

Embroider a flower onto front of each bootie, or attach a small bobble or pearl button as a decoration instead.

Mittens

Cast on 49 sts, work in garter st for 1⅜ in.

R1: k4, *k2tog, k6, rep from * 4 times more, k2tog, k3 = 43 sts.

R2: k3, m1 in next st, *k6, m1 in next st, rep from * 4 times more, k4 = 49 sts.

Work in garter st until work measures 4 in., then shape top.

Start row numbering again.

R1: *k2tog, k6, rep from * 5 times, k1 = 43 sts.

R2 and alternate rows: k.

R3: *k2tog, k5, rep from * 5 times more, k1 = 37 sts.

R5: *k2tog, k4, rep from * 5 times more, k1 = 31 sts.

R7: *k2tog, k3, rep from * 5 times more, k1 = 25 sts.

R9: *k2tog, k2, rep from * 5 times more, k1 = 19 sts.

R11: *k2tog, k1, rep from * 5 times more, k1 = 13 sts.

R13: *k2tog, rep from * 5 times more, k1 = 7 sts.

Thread yarn through remaining sts twice, then draw up. Cut thread, leaving tail long enough to sew seam.

Work another mitten in the same way.

Making up

Thread with ribbon at wrist or make a braid using some of the yarn (see p. 101).

Variation

Embroider a heart, flower, or other motif onto front of each mitten (see p. 68).

PATTERN SPECIFICATIONS:

- Yarn: fingering weight mercerized cotton 1 x 1-oz. ball
- Needles: #1 (2.25 mm)

Gauge: 34 sts/64 rows = 4 in. in garter st

Measurements: length 4¾ in.

Grade: 2

PATTERN SPECIFICATIONS:

- Yarn: fingering weight mercerized cotton 1 x 2-oz. ball

- Needles: #3 (3 mm) and crochet hook (optional)

Gauge: 30 sts/38 rows = 4 in. in st st

Measurements: diameter 14½ in.; depth 5 in. This project is designed to fit a newborn to three month old baby.

Grade: 3

Bonnet

Cast on 112 sts and work in garter stitch for ⅝ in., then work in st st until work measures 3 in.

Start top shaping (all garter st)
R1: *k12, k2tog, rep from * 7 times = 104 sts.
R2 and alternate rows: k.
R3: *k11, k2tog, rep from * 7 times = 96 sts.
R5: *k10, k2tog, rep from * 7 times = 88 sts.
R7: *k9, k2tog, rep from * 7 times = 80 sts.
R9: *k8, k2tog, rep from * 7 times = 72 sts.
R11: *k7, k2tog, rep from * 7 times = 64 sts.
R13: *k6, k2tog, rep from * 7 times = 56 sts.
R15: *k5, k2tog, rep from * 7 times = 48 sts.
R17: *k4, k2tog, rep from * 7 times = 40 sts.
R19: *k3, k2tog, rep from * 7 times = 32 sts.
R21: *k2, k2tog, rep from * 7 times = 24 sts.
R23: *k1, k2tog, rep from * 7 times = 16 sts.
Break off yarn, leaving a tail long enough to thread through remaining sts twice and, later, to sew side seam.

Earflaps

At hem edge and beg on 14th st from edge, pick up 26 sts. Then work these sts in garter st for ¾ in.
Start shaping.
R1 and alternate rows to R17: k2, k2tog, k to last 4 sts, k2tog, k2.
R2 and alternate rows: k.
R18: Bind off 8 stitches at end.
Make 2nd earflap, beg on 14th st from opposite end of hat. Work as first earflap. This makes a gap of 34 sts between each earflap.

Ties

Using the yarn doubled, make an 11-in. twisted braid (see page 101).
Alternatively, crochet an 11-in. chain or use a length of ribbon in a contrasting color. Sew securely at bottom edge of each earflap.

Making up

Sew side seam.

Variation

Embroider a chain stitch motif on front of bonnet.
Work blanket stitch around edge of hat or work earflaps and first ¾ in. of work in contrasting color.

Crib blanket

With MC, cast on 140 sts and follow graph, beg bottom right corner. Work seed st where indicated for border and st st everywhere else. Work to end, then bind off.

Each square (34 sts x 54 rows) is knitted using intarsia method. Do not pass the yarn across the back of work or weave it in, but work each square with a separate ball of yarn.

Finishing

Embroider chain st (see page 68) hearts on random squares.

Variations

Chain st the baby's name or date of birth at the top or bottom of the blanket.

Work a random square in seed or garter st.

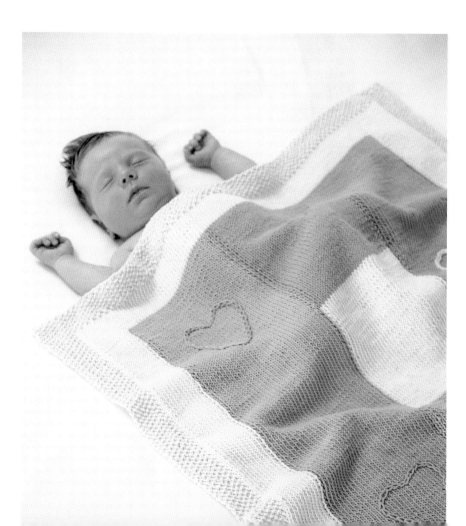

PATTERN SPECIFICATIONS:

- Yarn: sport weight cotton
  4 x 2-oz. balls MC; 2 x 2-oz.
  balls CC1, 2, and 3; 1 x 2-oz.
  ball CC4
- Needles: #6 (4 mm)

Gauge: 20 sts/29 rows = 4 in. in st st

Measurements: width 28 in.; length 35¾ in.

Grade: 4

Key:
MC = cream
CC1 = lilac
CC2 = pale pink
CC3 = pale blue
CC4 = pale green

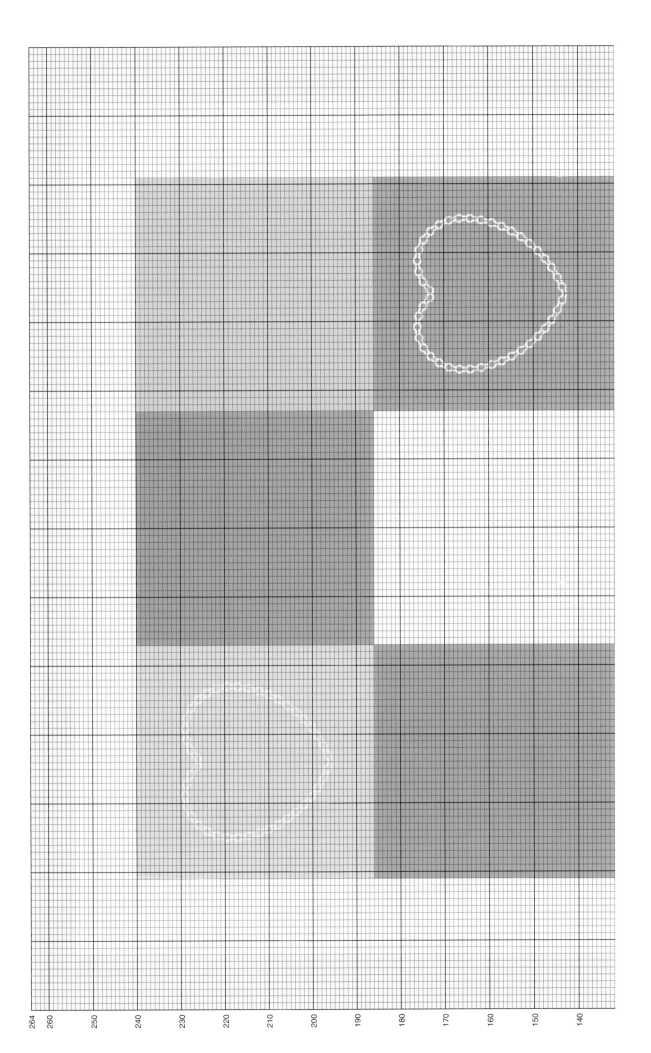

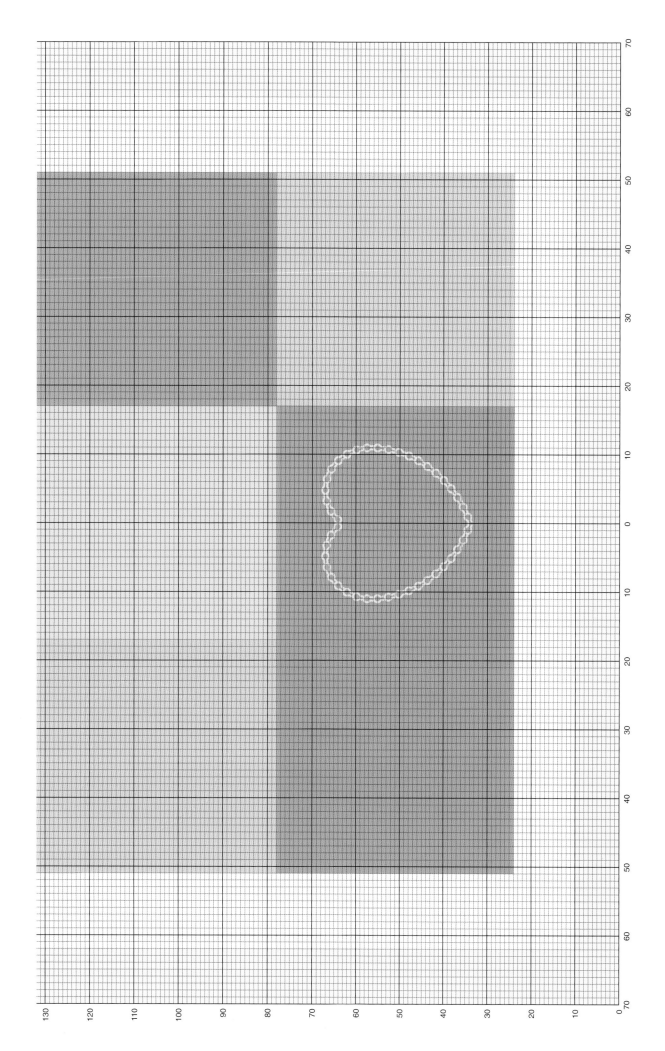

Baby cardigan

This cardigan opens at the back for easy dressing.

Front

With #2 (2.75 mm) needles, cast on 72 sts and work 8 rows garter st.
Change to #3 (3 mm) needles and work 30 rows st st, ending on a p row.
R39: k20, p32, k20.
R40: p20, k32, p20.
Rep R39–40 20 times more.
Work in st st for 20 rows.
Start neck shaping.
K30, turn, keeping rem 42 sts on st holder. Then dec 1 st on neck edge on following 6 rows (24 sts remain).
Decrease using fully fashioned method (working 3rd and 4th st from edge together). Then dec every alternate row 4 times more (20 sts remain). Continue in st st 5 rows more, then bind off.
Repeat neck, dec on opposite side as follows, rejoin yarn to remaining 30 sts at outside edge with RS facing, pick up 30 sts, leaving 12 sts across center on st holder. Work dec as given for first side.

1st back

With #2 (2.75 mm) needles, cast on 52 sts and work 8 rows in garter st. Change to #3 (3 mm) needles and work as follows:
R9: k.
R10: k6, p46.
Rep R9–10 for 111 rows. Bind off 20 sts and put 32 sts on st holder.

2nd back

With #2 (2.75 mm) needles, cast on 52 sts and work 8 rows in garter st. Change to #3 (3 mm) needles and work as follows:
R9: k.
R10: p46, k6.
Rep R9–10 for 111 rows. Put 32 sts on st holder, then bind off 20 sts.

Sleeves

With #2 (2.75 mm) needles, cast on 34 sts and work 8 rows in garter st. Change to #3 (3 mm) needles and cont in st st, inc 1 st at each end of next row and every 4th row until 66 sts, then work 10 rows more and cast off 66 sts.

PATTERN SPECIFICATIONS:

- Yarn: fingering mercerized cotton (can be matte fingering cotton) 6 x 2 oz.

- Needles: #2 (2.75 mm) and #3 (3 mm)

Gauge: 30 sts/38 rows = 4 in.

Measurements: width 9½ in.; length 12 in. This cardigan is for a child aged 3–6 months.

Grade: 4

Making up

Sew shoulder seams with a firm backstitch.

Neck band

With #2 (2.75 mm) needles, pick up 32 sts from first back, then pick up sts down front neck as follows: pick up *3 sts then miss next one * (this makes sure neck band stays flat), repeat * to * 3 times more, then pick up 3 sts and then 12 sts from st holder, pick up sts to match opposite front neck, then remaining 32 sts from back = 106 sts.
R1–3: k.
R4: k2, bind off 2 sts, k to last 4 sts, bind off 2 sts, k2 to end.
R5: k to end, casting on 2 sts over those bound off in R4.
R6–8: k.
Bind off.

Making up

Sew in sleeves to 5 in. below shoulder seam. Sew side seams of body and sleeves.
Sew a pearl button at either end of back neck close to shoulder point to match buttonholes.
Embroider a chain stitch heart in a contrasting color embroidery thread onto front on reverse st st square.

All sizes sweater

To adapt this pattern to fit any size—child or adult—figure out the width, finished length, and sleeve lengths that you require, then use the gauge to convert your measurements to stitches and rows. Use the section on designing and writing patterns to help.

This is the simplest and easiest shape possible to knit. If you would prefer a boat neck to the square neck, work a horizontal split at the center of the work.

Back and front
Cast on 60 sts and work in garter st for 8 in.
R1 and 2: cast on 32 sts, then k to end = 124 sts.
Cont in garter st until work measures 9½ in.

Start neck shaping.
R1: k 50 sts, putting rem 74 sts on st holder.
Turn and work garter st on these 50 sts for 2½ in. more, ending on outside edge of work.
Transfer these sts to another st holder, then pick up 74 sts from 1st st holder. Beg at neck edge, bind off 24 sts and work garter st on rem 50 sts for 2½ in. more, ending on outside edge of work.
On next row, k50, cast on 24 sts, then work 50 sts from st holder. Work garter st on these 124 sts until work measures 16 in.
Bind off 32 sts at beg of next 2 rows, then work garter st on 60 sts until work measures 23½ in., and bind off.

Making up
Fold garment over and sew side seams of sleeves and body.

To finish
Use a contrasting color yarn to work blanket stitch around hem and cuff edges and neck (optional).

Variations
Use different colors for blanket st at neck, cuff, and hem.
Try knitting in garter st stripes.

PATTERN SPECIFICATIONS:

- Yarn: sport weight wool 4 x 2-oz. balls.
- Needles: #6 (4 mm)

Gauge: 20 sts/38 rows = 4 in. in garter st

Measurements: width 11½ in.; length 12 in.

Grade: 1

Sailor sweater

This sweater comes in two sizes: 3–5 years and 5–7 years. It would be very easy to adapt to other sizes, as the body is made up of two squares and the sleeves could be shortened or lengthened as needed.

For Quaker ridge pattern:
R1, 3, 5, 6, 7, 9, 11, 12, 14 (RS): k.
R2, 4, 8, 10, 13: p.
Rep R1–14.

Front and back

With CC1 and #4 (3.25 mm) needles, cast on 77 (87) sts.
Change to MC and work 8 rows garter st.
Change to #6 (4 mm) needles and follow Quaker ridge pattern, working rows 1–4 and 7–10 in MC and rows 5–6 and 11–14 in CC2.
Cont until work measures 14½ (17¾) in., ending on an MC row on R4 or R10 of pattern.
Cont with MC, working 1½ in. in garter st.
Change to CC1 and bind off.

Sleeves

With CC1 and #3 (3.25 mm) needles, cast on 40 (44) sts, then change to MC and work 8 rows in garter st. Change to #6 (4 mm) needles and follow Quaker ridge pattern as for front and back, inc 1 st at either end of next row and every 6th row until 66 (72) sts. Cont until sleeve measures 13¾ (15¾) in., ending on an MC row. Bind off.

Making up

Sew shoulder seams with CC1, leaving an 8¼- (9-) in. gap for neck, though note that this will vary depending on head size of child. It is therefore best to pin shoulder seams with knitting pins, tack them, and then try sweater on child.
Sew in sleeves to 6¾ (7½) in. below shoulder seam, slightly stretch sleeve head to this measurement, and sew side seams.

Variations

Leave a side split by beg side seam above first 8 rows of garter st at hem.
Add a third color to garter ridges to make a more colorful garment.

PATTERN SPECIFICATIONS:

- Yarn: sport weight cotton
  4 x 2-oz. balls MC and CC2;
  1 x 1-oz. ball CC1
- Needles: #3 (3.25 mm) and
  #6 (4 mm)

Gauge: 20 sts/30 rows = 4 in. in Quaker ridge pattern

Measurements: width 14⅛ (16⅛) in.; length 16⅜ (19½) in.

Grade: 2

Key:
MC = navy
CC1 = red
CC2 = natural

PATTERN SPECIFICATIONS:

- Yarn: sport weight cotton
  7 x 2-oz. balls
- Needles: #6 (4 mm) and
  #3 (3.25 mm)

Gauge: 20 sts/26 rows = 4 in. in
st st

Measurements: length 21⅝ (24)
in.; chest 26 (29⅛) in.

Grade: 3

Pinafore

This dress comes in two sizes: 2–4 yrs and 4–6 yrs.

Back

With #3 (3.25 mm) needles, cast on 95 (103) sts and work in st st for 1¼ in.,
ending on a p row.
Make a row of eyelets as follows: k1, *yfd, k2tog, rep from * to end.
Cont in st st for 1¼ in. more. This forms the picot edge. At this point you can
either work together st for st: 1 st from the cast-on row with 1 st from the
needle, and pick up the hem this way, or you can wait until the end and catch
stitch the hem in place.

Change to #3 (4 mm) needles and cont in st st until work measures 14⅛ (15¾)
in., ending on a WS row. Change to #4 (3.25 mm) needles and cont in k1, p1 rib
as follows:
R1: k1, p2tog, then work tog every 3rd and 4th st in rib to last 3 sts, p2tog, k1 =
71 (77) sts.
Cont in rib for 17 (19) more rows.

Start armhole shaping.
R1: bind off 2 sts at beg of next 6 rows, then dec 1 st at beg of following 6 rows
= 53 (59) sts.
Cont in rib until work measures 21¾ (24) in., then bind off all sts.

Pocket

With #6 (4 mm) needles, cast on 23 sts and work 32 rows in st st. Change to #4
(3.25 mm) needles and work in k1, p1 rib for 6 rows, then bind off.

Front

Work as back to top of hem, change to #6 (4 mm) needles, then work 44 rows
more in st st, ending on a p row, and attach pocket as follows:
Beg on 24th st from left side, k cast-on edge of pocket with the following 23 sts,
then cont to end. Cont in st st until work measures 14⅛ (15¾) in., ending on a k
row. Change to #4 (3.25 mm) needles.
R1: k1, p2tog, then work tog every 3rd and 4th st in rib to last 4 sts, k1, p2tog,
k1 = 71 (77) sts.
Work in rib for 17 (19) rows, then shape armhole as on back and continue until
25 (33) rows of rib have been worked.

Start front neck shaping.
R1 (RS): Cast off 11 (15) sts across center of work. Then, working one side at a
time:
R2: bind off 3 (4) sts on neck edge.

R3: rib.

R4: bind off 2 sts at neck edge.

Dec 1 st on neck edge every alternate row 5 times = 11 sts.

Then rib until work measures 22¾ (25⅛) in. Bind off 11 sts.

Begin working opposite side, starting at neck edge. Decrease as for neck shaping above.

Making up

Sew 11 bound-off stitches from front shoulder to 11 bound-off stitches from back piece. Sew side seams, sewing in all ends. Sew sides of pocket following a vertical line of sts. The front is 2 in. longer than the back so that the shoulder seams lies down the back, slightly lowering the back neck away from the nape of the neck.

Embroider a chain stitch motif onto the pocket, butterfly, flower or heart are a few examples (see page 68).

Making a picot hem

1 Cast on an odd number of stitches. Work in stockinette stitch for the depth of the hem edge, ending on a purl row. On the next row, make a row of holes by working k1, yfd, k2tog, to the end of the row. Then work in stockinette stitch for the same number of rows from the cast-on edge to the row of holes.

2 Turn up the hem and sew it with a catch stitch. (This is where you catch up a hem by picking up one stitch from either side of the work, where the cast-on edge meets the row of knitted fabric it is being sewn to. The stitch is worked diagonally with a darning needle and thread, as in hemming in needlework.) Alternatively, knit up the hem by knitting together one stitch from the needle with one loop from the cast-on edge by putting the loop from the cast-on edge onto the left needle and knitting it together with the next stitch.

part

5

DESIGN

INSPIRATION

The knitting process is very exciting and creative because not only are you creating a garment, as you would with sewing, but you are also creating the fabric itself—from nothing more than a length of thread. If you are also designing the fabric and garment yourself, then knitting becomes extremely fulfilling creatively because you have devised a unique piece of work.

Everyone designs in a different way with a huge selection of starting points. Many things can trigger ideas, but experience—knowing what works and what doesn't, which comes from years of designing knitwear—is my biggest influence as a knitwear designer. Since experience cannot be taught, here is a list of some starting points that may inspire you.

New yarn

When you see a new yarn that attracts you—whether it is the color or texture that appeals—you may feel that you just have to turn it into something. This can be the starting point for a new garment.

Ideas notebook

Keep a notebook for ideas so that you can record anything you like whenever you see it. Sketch garment shapes, patterns, and motifs—anything that jumps out at you—and tear pictures out of magazines. Saving them all in your notebook means that you have plenty of inspiration for starting points for your own designs. Then, when you see a yarn that you like, you can refer to your notebook and see if there is anything there that would translate well using this new fiber.

Old patterns

Old knitting patterns can be another great source of inspiration: update something by knitting it in a contemporary yarn or change the needle size and see what the results are. Creating a unique garment in this way can be relatively easy, and this process of adaptation will inspire you to develop your design skills more.

Vintage patterns are often available in thrift stores, and whether they are from the 1940s or 1970s, they will be full of inspiration. Look at them for shape ideas or simply for stitch reference, and if you spot an unusual stitch texture, write it down so that you can transform it into an original design of your own. Do not be deterred by the type of yarn or colors that are used, as these will inevitably look dated. Try instead to see beyond that and use your imagination to extract something for your own design work. These old patterns will help you to see the capabilities of different yarns and stitches, which make them design starting points that are rich in reference.

Finally, color combinations or patterns, pictures torn out of old magazines, and historical costume books can also be sources of inspiration for a designer.

DESIGNING YOUR OWN

From the changing colors of the trees through the seasons to some graffiti on a rusty metal door—all sorts of colors, shapes, and textures can influence your creative thoughts. Keep a notebook for swatches and tear sheets to track your ideas.

If you see a lovely flower, you could simply draw it, then make a graph of your design and knit it straight onto a new sweater. In this way, you would be using the whole image as your influence—the shape, color, texture, and proportions of one thing would have inspired your latest knitted design. Alternatively, you could try to disassociate the image from what it actually is and try instead to extract the part that you can use in your work, for example, the shape of the stamen, the form of the leaf veins, or the color of the petals.

The importance of color

Nature is probably the most clever and creative user of color. Next time you see a flower, tree, or stone that you like, ask yourself what it is that appeals to you and look closely at the different colors, noting if they change at different times of the day. Use colored pencils or paints to try and capture that combination. You will probably find that it is the ratio of colors next to each other that draws the eye in.

Making a color palette

As a starting point for making your own color palette, use strips of colored paper or colored areas cut out from magazines. Place them together, playing around with the proportions, seeing what happens when one color is next to or on top of another. Then move onto knitting striped sample swatches, using these colors as a starting point. Changing the dominating color will dramatically alter the look of your sample: it can seem warmer or cooler and even have a mood, happy or sad. Color evokes emotion, reminding you of a time past in the same way that smell does. That is why we associate certain decades with different color combinations.

Color forecasting

Professional color trends affect us all, whether we realize it or not. Every manufacturing industry, not just fashion, uses color forecasting experts to inform them of the changing trends in colors. That is why it is not just coincidence that automobile companies all produce very similar colors for their latest styles at the same time or that the latest household linens are all based around the same tone of pink or blue in one season. These color trends have been set down a few years earlier by color teams whose job it is to explore and develop color themes for a living. What direction is society going in? What is influencing young people at the moment? The color forecasters have to answer these questions and predict the trends before they happen.

Mood boards

At the beginning of each design season, professional designers create mood boards—combinations of magazine tear sheets, postcards, beautiful images from anywhere, yarn wrappings and fabric swatches, blocks of color, and whatever else appeals to their aesthetic nature. Each board is then given a name to evoke a feeling that the designer wishes to convey; even the title will conjure up yet another visual image in the mind's eye.

You can create your own mood board in the same way, collecting images that you like—images that say something to you—then using these ideas to develop your knitwear designs. A simpler experiment would be to find a postcard that you like and then try to find yarns that match the colors used in the image. Knit simple stripes, changing the widths until you get the color combination that appeals to you.

Color in art

Try looking at color trends from other cultures around the world; visit museums and concentrate on one or two areas that particularly appeal to you. It may be the Egyptian section or the antique textiles room. Look closely at the exhibits and ask yourself why you are drawn to one particular item. Then figure out what you can take from that piece to put into your own design.

Paintings are another endless source of color influence and inspiration. They contain huge clues as to where the artist was painting. For example, the work of Frida Kahlo could not be portraying anything but Mexico, and the Italian Renaissance artists set even religious scenes in a Tuscan landscape. The colors used in many paintings relate to the artist's surroundings, so both the image and the color are important as an influence for your own work. Abstract contemporary art is another great way of learning about color combinations.

Colors around the world

Color and design are intertwined, and all countries have their own color identity. These differences are often associated with the light quality in each area: for example, northern European colors are very different from African colors. Advertising billboards interpret a country's individual color identity, so the same poster design in South America would use very different colors if it was used in eastern Europe, and it would be different again if used in Asia.

Travel books can show you how different countries combine colors to convey their color identity in ways you would not have thought possible. Perhaps looking at color through the eyes of a different culture will inspire you to mix colors in a way you had never considered before.

Experimenting with stitches

The stitch library in this book is only the tip of the iceberg, and any one of these patterns will look completely different when knitted in different yarns.

You can also experiment with different needle sizes, which will make your work tighter or looser. Try knitting a single yarn type, starting with a tight gauge, then working through four or five needle sizes until the stitches are large and loopy. The swatch will have widened considerably by the end, but it will demonstrate the design potential you have using simple stockinette stitch and experimenting with the needles. You could even use this method to create a garment that flares at the hem or cuffs without using any increasing for the shaping, which would be done simply by changing needle sizes.

Using different yarns

To see just how versatile stitches and yarns can be, try an experiment by working from just one of the stitch patterns. Collect together various yarn types—wool, cotton, and rayon, in sock yarn to bulky thickness—then work the same swatch using these matte and shiny, thick and thin, smooth and rough yarns. Each one will look very different, and this experiment will help you to realize the endless combinations with which you could chose to work.

Designing a garment

There are standard styles that are always popular in knitwear and this is due to the nature of a knitted fabric. Unlike woven materials, the construction and elasticity of knitwear can often mean that complicated shapes will not work unless backed with a firm woven fabric or by using complicated seam taping. It is best to go with the nature of knitting rather than going against it.

Below and right Inspiration can come from many sources: trips to museums, a walk in the woods, or travels abroad.

Designing your garment

For your first knitted design, choose a simple style, letting the yarn, the color, or the stitch type be the design feature. If you start with something too complicated, you might be deterred from further attempts, whereas success with a simple pattern will encourage you to advance to more complicated ones later on.

A drop-shoulder style is an obvious one to choose, because it needs no shaping on the sleeve head or body, making it very straightforward. Since such a sleeve is a fairly easy shape to design, you could take the opportunity to experiment with the sleeve shape itself. This could be wide, narrow, cropped, extra long and slim, or flared at the end using simple edge decreasing.

For the top of the garment, choose a simple round neck, as this will be easier to achieve than a V-neck. For the bottom, decide whether you want a hem edge or rib. You also need to decide whether there will be any fastenings on the garment, and, if so, whether you want buttons, a zipper, or ties.

You could also add a simple design feature, such as a patch pocket, to give interest. This doesn't have to be placed on the front of the garment—you could make a small pocket to go on the top of a sleeve. Adding some embroidery to your garment later is also a way of designing something that is clever and intricate-looking but easy to knit.

When designing for yourself, look at the knitwear that you like and ask yourself what it is that appeals to you about that piece. Is it the shape, the stitch, the weight and yarn type, the color? Use your answers to help you design new garments for yourself.

Working a gauge swatch

When designing your own knitwear, you will probably begin by seeing a yarn that you would love to use. If you have reached this stage, you will also have an idea of what that yarn may look like when knitted up. But the first step is to try out the stitches and decide on the needle size. Work a few swatches until you have the fabric texture that looks right for you. There is usually a needle size recommended on the yarn ball band, but with time you will learn which needles work with which yarns.

Having chosen the yarn, stitch, and needle combination, the next stage is to work your gauge swatch (see page 29). This is the key to getting the size of garment you want. As you are not working to anyone else's designs, you can simply work swatches until you are happy with the look.

Measure your stitches and rows over a 4-in. square, then use this to work out your pattern. It is also important to remember that different stitches produce different gauges; for example, seed stitch spreads a lot more than stockinette stitch, while cables will draw in your work. This is vital information when working out patterns and designing your own knitwear. If your garment is to be mostly seed stitch, do not work out your pattern from a stockinette stitch swatch, as it will come out much wider than expected. If a cable pattern is what you want, then use a cable swatch for your gauge.

Measuring and drawing your garment

After you've researched your color themes, chosen your yarn, designed your garment, and decided what type of stitches you want to use, you can begin the measuring and drawing processes.

Measuring

Whatever your pattern, you will need to be very organized and have all your measurements at hand along with paper (some people may also need knitters' graph paper), pencils, eraser, and the all-important calculator.

If you haven't worked from your own pattern before, start with a simple shape to get the principles right. You could use an old, favorite sweater as a template for the measurements. If you know that the shape suits you and the size is right, this is probably a good idea as a starting point.

Measure from the center back neck to cuff. Beginning at the top of where the spine would be, go along the shoulder and down the arm, with the arm at the side, as this is the longest point. Also measure the armhole depth from shoulder to underarm, and the cuff width. Record all these measurements on your drawing.

Decide on the depth of the neckline at the front and back and also the width of the neck. If you are attaching a neckband, take this into account.

If you are being more ambitious and starting from

scratch, the same principles apply, but you need to have a very well thought out design and drawing with all the measurements written on it. You will also need to take the measurements from yourself, as you will not have a template garment. Remember to allow for movement in the garment and a small seam allowance.

Drawing

Draw a plan of your garment on a piece of paper, marking all the measurements you have in the right place. You now need to convert these measurements to stitches and rows.

If the width of your garment is to be 20 in. and your gauge swatch is 20 stitches to 4 in. (five stitches per inch), then you need to cast on 100 stitches. Work out all the horizontal measurements and record them on your drawing. Then do the same for all the vertical measurements, converting the lengths to rows in the same way. For example, if your gauge is 32 rows to 4 in. (eight rows per inch), then to knit ¾ in. you would need six rows.

This is why the gauge swatch is so crucial. If your gauge swatch doesn't match your gauge on the garment, even if it is off by only 1 stitch every 2 in., it can make a huge difference to the finished size of your work over the width or length of your garment.

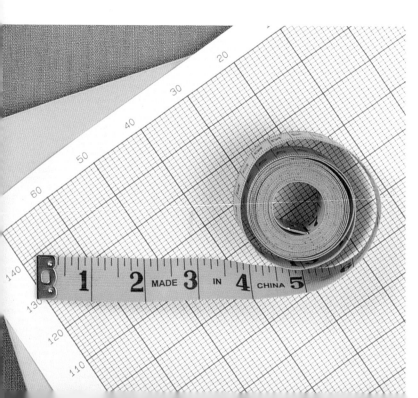

CREATING GRAPHS AND PATTERNS

You may find that using a graph is a much easier way to figure out your pattern shaping than going straight into writing a pattern, and working from graphs is essential if you are knitting a motif. A beginner may find it easier to figure out decreasings and increasings on graph paper, as each stitch and row is represented by a square. In fact, I would recommend this for a first-time pattern writer.

Graphs

Knitters' graph paper is available from specialty stores. A stitch is wider than it is long, and to reflect this, each square on knitters' graph paper is more oblong than square to give an accurate interpretation when drawing up a motif. Although it is possible to work patterns on ordinary graph paper, you must remember that your work will appear elongated, which can be very distracting.

Starting with the front measurements, you need to draw the outline of your garment on graph paper, using each square to represent a stitch. If your garment is, for example, to be 100 stitches wide and 130 rows long, mark these measurements as an outline on the paper, using a pencil so that you can erase any errors. Next, mark the graph at the points where you want to have shaping, usually the neck and maybe the armhole, unless it is to be a drop shoulder. Mark the width of the back neck and the depth of the front neck measurements on the graph, referring to your drawing for the number of rows and stitches that relate to these measurements. With a light pencil, draw a curve connecting these points. Then outline the neck edge using the edge of the squares to show where to decrease.

If you are knitting a simple garment, you may find that you can draw the back on the front graph, using a contrast color to outline the back neck shaping. Repeat the process, making a graph for the sleeves and for any other pieces.

When you are knitting, follow these graphs along with a written pattern that gives all the essential information—gauge, needle sizes, yarn, number of stitches to cast on, etc. Add any other information you think necessary.

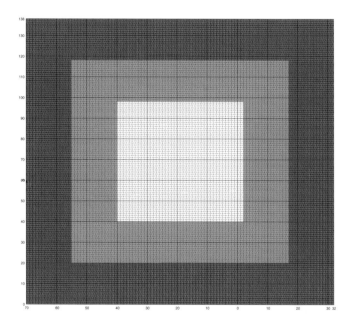

Motifs on graphs To design a motif into your work, make a graph as above with all the shaping details in place. Draw or trace the motif required on the graph, then draw around the edge, converting the shape into squares (stitches). If the motif is made up of more than one color, fill in each square using different symbols, one for each color; for larger sections, use colored pencils to fill in the areas or simply write a number to represent each color inside the different areas. Be sure to make a note of your symbols/key on the written part of your design.

If you are knitting words into your design, remember that you must start at the bottom right-hand corner of the graph to ensure that the words appear correctly.

Patterns

You may find it useful to refer to a simple pattern in this book as a starting point, writing your own pattern with this as a template. Having outlined the gauge and what equipment is required, give instructions for the first row, e.g., "With #7 (4.5 mm) needles and MC, cast on 100 sts and work in k1, p1 rib for 2 in." Remember that if you are having a rib at the start of your garment, this will usually be knitted on smaller-size needles than the main body. Therefore the pattern would start after the rib with a change to larger needles. You then continue knitting in the correct stitch until a point where you may have to start shaping the garment.

Adding shaping To figure this out, you need to subtract the number of stitches you are decreasing to from the original number of stitches. For example, let's say you have 100 stitches at the chest, and after decreasing for the armholes, you want to be left with 80 stitches. You should have a vertical measurement from the underarm to the point where the decreasing would finish, and you should have converted this from inches to rows and noted it on your drawing. Using this measurement—let's say 30 rows —this will mean that you have to lose the 20 stitches over 30 rows by decreasing on the outside edge of your work. Don't forget that decreasing is mostly done at both ends of your work, so losing 20 stitches over 30 rows will mean decreasing 10 stitches at either end of the garment. Simply divide 30 by 10 and this will tell you that you need to decrease one stitch at both ends of every third row.

This is the basic principle of figuring out a pattern, but, as with all principles, there is a huge amount of variation involved, which will depend on the types of shaping you want. You will, therefore, need to have a clear idea of what kind of angles you require in your work. You might want to decrease with a sharp angle at first, then more gradually, or you might prefer a gentle, even decrease. Wherever you want your shaping and whatever angle it is at—whether its increasing or decreasing—you use the same principle of dividing stitches into rows.

CARING FOR KNITWEAR

You will also want to look after your garment properly, using suitable washing and storage methods. After all your hard work, it would be a shame to spoil your creation by neglecting the proper washing and storing procedures.

Washing knitwear

Always wash handmade knitwear with care. Modern yarns are always tried and tested and many of them can be machine washed, but always check the washing instructions on the ball band and follow them carefully. Most washing machines have special cycles for woolens and delicates that protect fibers from being weakened by too much friction and heat. As a result of this, not too much hand-washing is needed today, although you may prefer this method—certainly for your finer knitwear.

Hand-washing If you are in any doubt, hand-wash items using gentle soap flakes. Do not leave the garments to soak. Instead, wash them gently and then rinse repeatedly until the water is clear. Never rub garments: wool may felt, and although cotton is tougher, it may pill if rubbed too aggressively.

Once the garment has been thoroughly rinsed, squeeze out the excess water gently, without wringing or twisting the garment. Then roll the knitwear in a thick towel to remove excess water and repeat until you have removed as much water as possible. Alternatively, put the garment in a pillowcase and use the short-spin setting on the washing machine.

Testing for colorfastness Most yarns will be colorfast, but if you are not sure, dip a small piece into soapy water and press it on a white cloth. If it leaves a stain, wash it in cold water on its own.

Drying Dry all knitted items, whether hand- or machine-washed, flat on either a towel or a clotheshorse, away from direct heat. If after all this care your garment has been distorted, try steaming it back into shape.

Storage

Avoid hanging your knitwear on coat hangers, as this will stretch and pull them out of shape. Instead, always fold them and put them in a drawer. If you have pure wool garments, store them with some kind of moth deterrent —lavender bags or cedar wood balls seem to work well.

If you do find moth holes, repair them, if possible, then have the garment dry-cleaned or put it in a plastic bag in the freezer for twenty-four hours—both these methods should kill any larvae. Clean the storage area thoroughly and put moth deterrent in it. A good idea is to store knitwear in sealed bags during seasons when they are not being worn regularly.

Conversion Charts

Knitting needle sizes

In an ideal world, we would have a standardized system worldwide for measurements and, especially, knitting needles. However, many countries have established their own idea of gauges. In Europe, the metric system is mostly used. This has the advantage of being a direct measurement of the the width of the needle. The old British system and the American version use random numbers. The best way to solve any problems with identifying old or unmarked needles is to keep a needle gauge in your knitting bag. That way you will be able to convert patterns with ease.

mm	U.S./Can #	Old UK/Can Sizes
2	0	14
2.25	1	13
2.75	2	12
3		11
3.25	3	10
3.75	5	9
4	6	8
4.5	7	7
5	8	6
5.5	9	5
6	10	4
6.5	10.5	3
7		2
7.5		1
8	11	0
9	13	00
10	15	000

Tip
• Ultimately you should aim to have a complete selection of needles of every size. Once you have several pairs, a special needle roll is recommended to store them all neatly. Make your own from a rectangle of fabric with two bands to hold the needles in place. Then the whole thing can be rolled up for storage.
• Circular needles can be particularly difficult to keep in order. Keep them in separate bags marked with their size, or make another holder for them that can be hung up.

Abbreviations

At their simplest, the abbreviations used on knitting patterns and in knitting books are shortened words or letters acting as shorthand for simple instructions, such as "rep" (repeat) and "k1" (knit one stitch). More complicated abbreviations, such as "psso" (pass slipped stitch over) will explain how to perform knitting methods. Most abbreviations are standard throughout all patterns, and many of them are obvious, but occasionally you will come across ones that you have not seen before. These will have been devised as ways of achieving specific tasks. It is therefore always worth familiarizing yourself with the abbreviations before you start.

beg	begin/beginning
CC	contrasting color
cable back	Hold dpn at back of work.
cable front	Hold dpn in front of work.
cont	continue
dec	decrease/decreasing (knit two stitches together)
dpn	double-pointed needle, also known as "cable needle," and used for cabling
inc	increase/increasing
inc in next st	Knit into the front and then into the back of the same stitch.
K	knit
k2tog	Knit two stitches together as one stitch.
kwise	knitwise
m1	Make one. Knit into the front of the stitch in the usual way, then, without discarding the stitch (which is still on the left needle), knit into the back of it to make two stitches.
MC	Main color.
P	purl
patt	Work in pattern.
p2tog	Purl two stitches together as one stitch.
psso	pass slipped stitch over. Insert the left needle into the stitch that has just been slipped and then draw this stitch to the left—over the stitch just knitted and over the end of the right needle and off.
pwise	purlwise
R	row
rem	remain/remaining
rep	repeat
rib	Usually means k1, p1 rib or whatever rib has been used in the pattern so far.
RS	right side

sl	Slip stitch (pass a stitch onto the opposite needle without knitting it). Slip kwise if a knit row and pwise if a purl row.
slip marker	Slip stitch marker from where you initially placed it onto row you are now working.
ssk	Slip, slip, knit. Slip the first then the second stitches kwise, then insert the left needle into the fronts of these two stitches from the left, and knit them together in this position. This makes a knit form of decrease.
st	stitch
st holder	stitch holder
st st	stockinette stitch
sts	stitches
tog	together
WS	wrong side
wyif	With yarn in front. When a stitch is slipped, the yarn is carried across in front of the stitch, so the yarn is on the side of the needles toward the knitter.
wyib	with yarn in back
yb	Yarn back. Take yarn to the back of the needle.
yfd	yarn forward. Bring yarn to the front of the needle.
yon	yarn over needle
yrn	yarn round needle
Grade	**1** = easy **2** = may include simple shaping **3** = medium ability **4** = for confident knitters **5** = may require understanding of color changing, stitch patterns, and/or more complicated shaping

Suppliers

Acknowledgments

The publisher would like to thank the following companies for supplying materials for the photography.

Furniture: Emily Readett-Bayley
Emily Readett-Bayley Tel: 44 (0)1400 281563
www.emilyreadettbayley.com

Yarn: Dyed in The Wool
Cliffe End Business Park, Dale Street,
Londwood, Huddersfield, HD3 4TG, UK
Tel: 44 (0)7899 794179
Fax: 44 (0)1484 716011
www.dyedinthewool.co.uk

Yarn: Copley Marshall and Co.
Wildspur Mills, New Mill, Huddersfield,
West Yorkshire, England HD7 7ET, UK
Fax: 44 (0)1484 684970

Yarn: Texere Yarns
College Mill, Texere, Barkerend Road,
Bradford, West Yorkshire, BD1 4AU, UK
Tel: 44 (0)1274 722191
Fax: 44 (0)1274 393500
Email: info@texere.co.uk
www.texere.co.uk

Yarn Web sites

This is by no means an exhaustive list, but every site will have links to another—so go surf and knit!

www.theknittinggarden.com
Beautiful assortment of yarns.

www.rowanyarns.co.uk
Fantastic designs for garments and accessories from Rowan's designers, including international suppliers.

www.kaleidosopeyarns.com
Yarns, kits, and knitting accessories.

www.tkga.com
The Knitting Guild Association, featuring knitting events and organizations.

www.castoff.info
Fabulous designs and knitting with attitude. Chat room in which to meet other knitters.

www.jklneedles.com
Unusual and hard-to-find knitting supplies.

www.shetland-wool-brokers.zetnet.co.uk
Mail-order suppliers of Shetland Wool, yarn, lace, raw fleece, and hand knitting accessories.

www.yarnsinternational.com
A wide selection of top-quality yarn; a full range of colors and weights.

www.theyarnco.com
New York–based knitting supplies company.

www.sweetgrasswool.com
Stocks 100% pure wool grown in Montana from Targhee sheep fleece.

www.knitr2.com
On-line magazine and supplier of unique yarns that can be knitted, tied, glued, written on, and stapled.

www.knitty.com
Canadian magazine full of original ideas, patterns, and links to suppliers and knitting blogs.

www.stitchnbitch.org
The home of Stitch 'n Bitch Chicago. Link up to knitting circles and clubs internationally.

www.yarn.com
Yarns, kits, knitting tools, and information on knitting courses and classes.

Knitters' graph paper

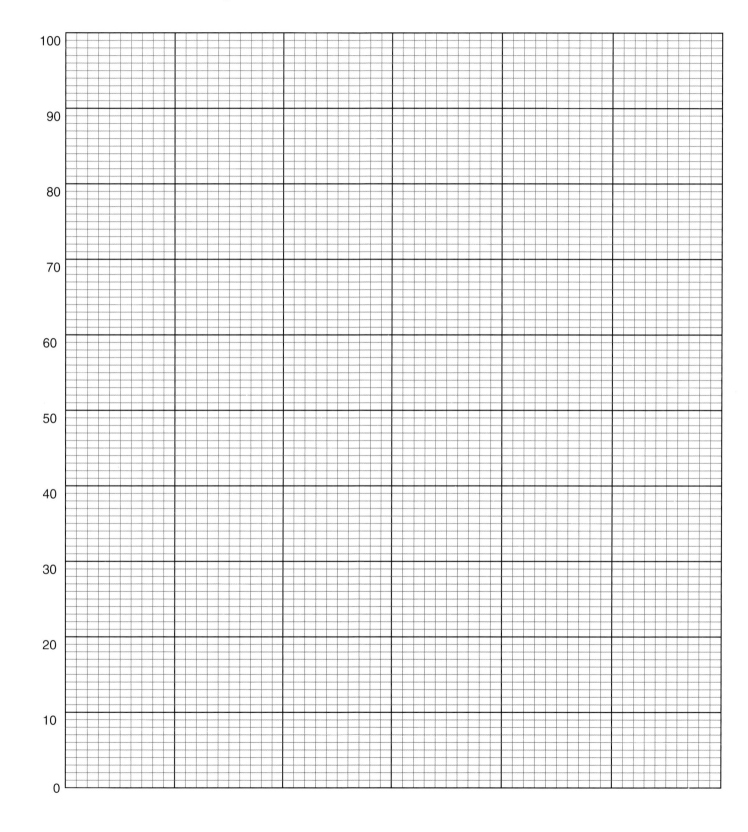

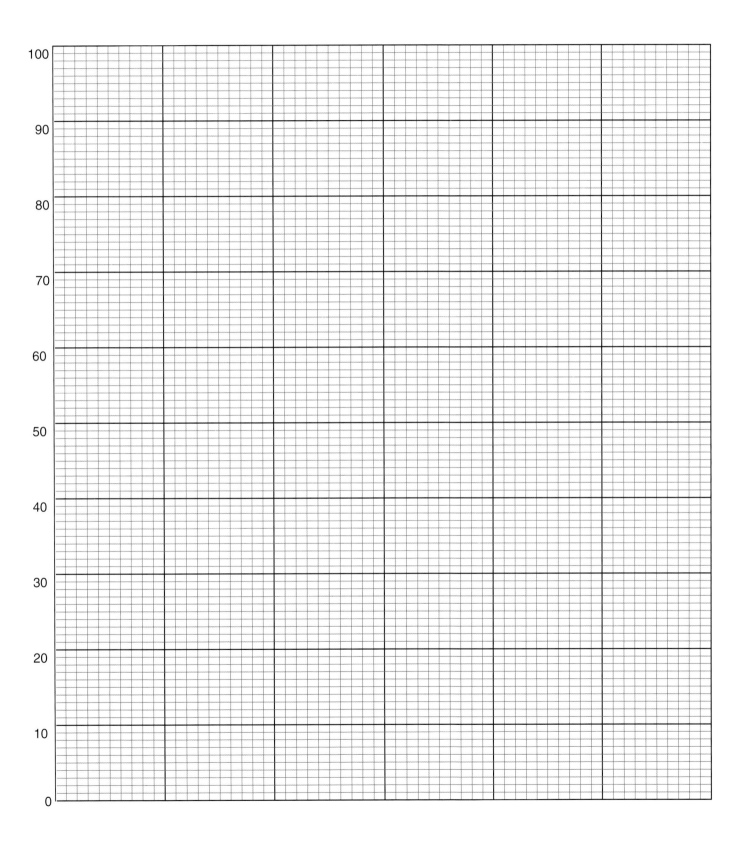

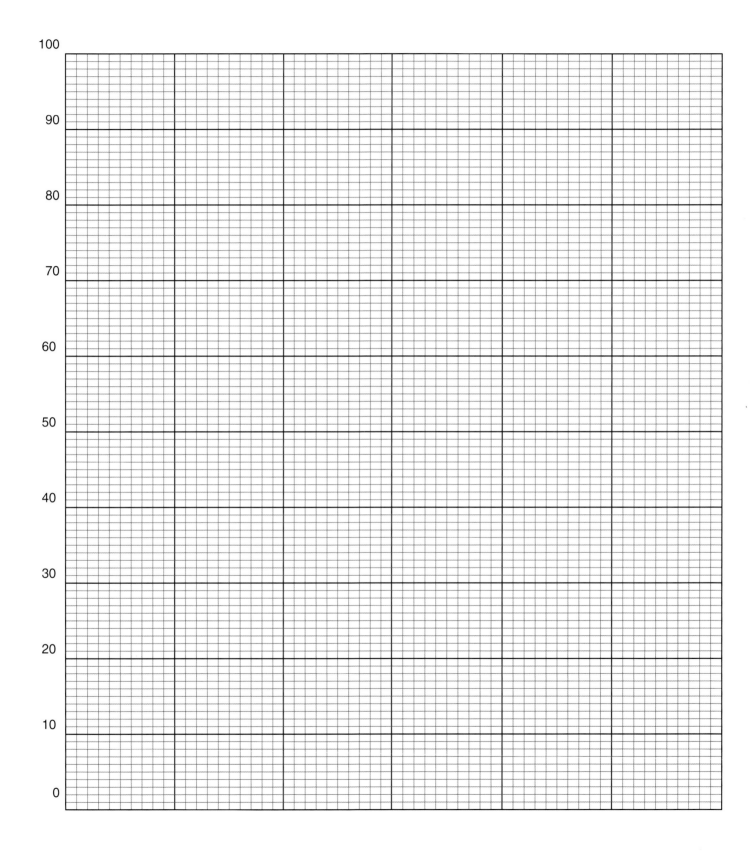

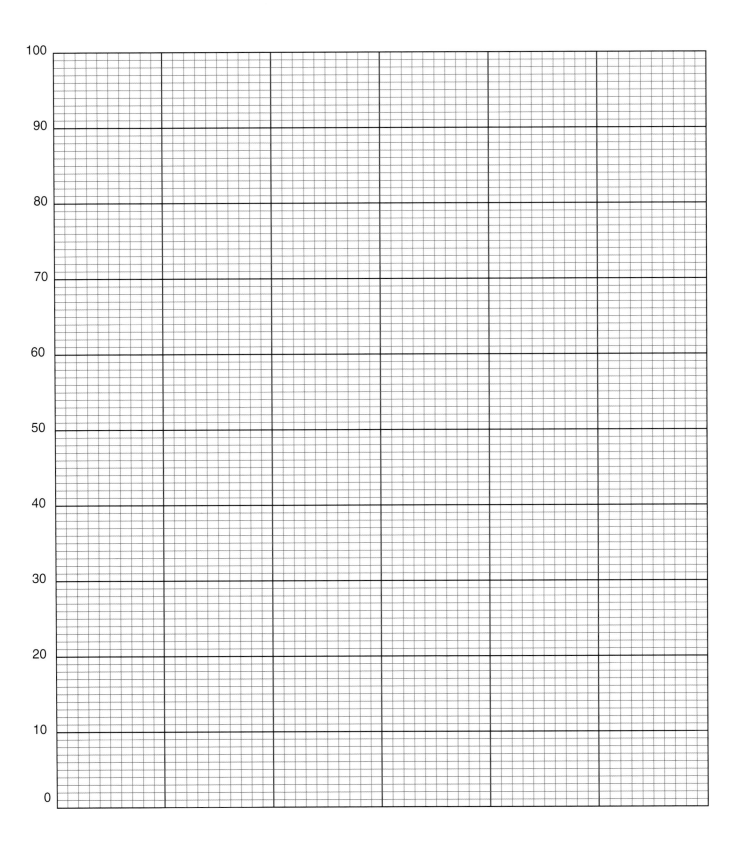

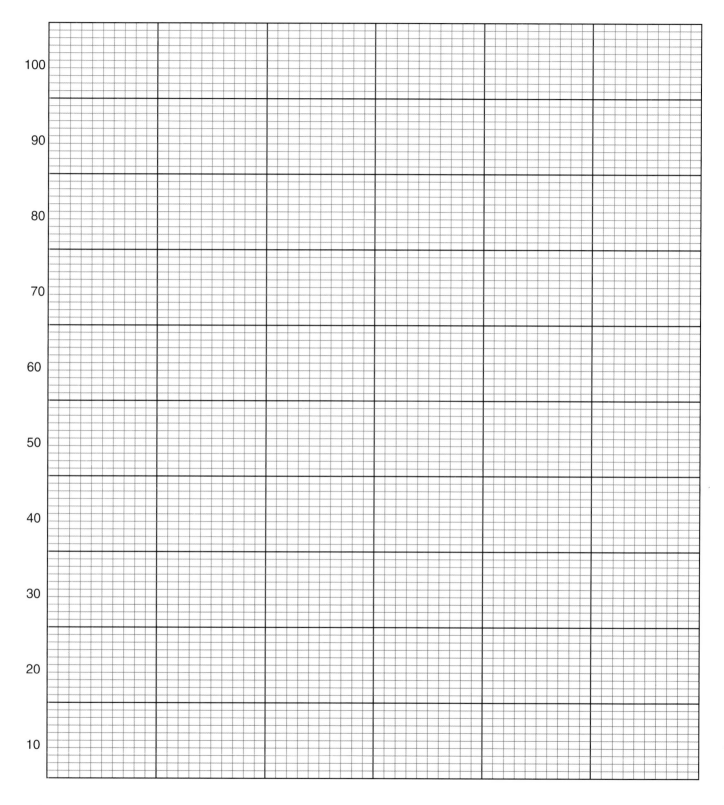

100

90

80

70

60

50

40

30

20

10

0

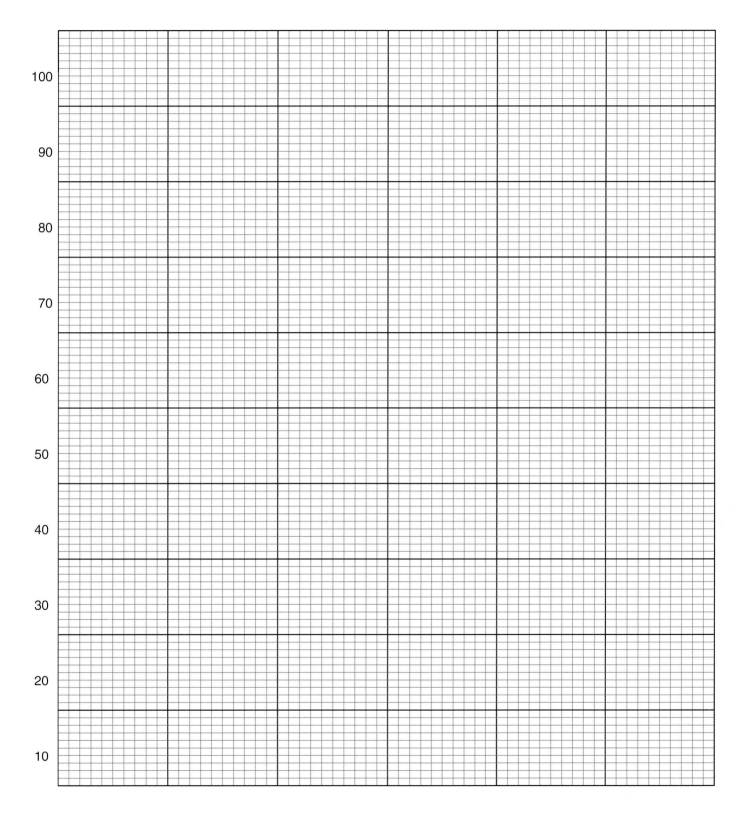

INDEX

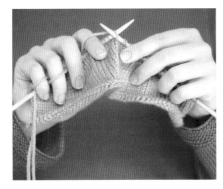

Author's acknowledgments

Thank you to Ben, Martha, and Ceidra.

Thanks also to all knitters everywhere who are keeping the craft alive, but especially Monica McMillan, Mary Williams, Ruth Badger, Rita Box, Mrs. Spalding, Thelma German, and Joan Hirst.

Thanks to Lizzie Orme and Catherine Huckerby for the lovely photography. Thanks also to the editor, Katy Bevan, and the pattern checker, Marilyn Wilson, and everyone else involved with the production of this book.